MONEY MANAGEMENT WITH ***QUICKEN***

Jean Miles

NOTE TO THE READER

Keystrokes to entered are enclosed in square braces '[]' and printed in `courier bold.`

For example:

`[Ctrl] - [Enter]` indicates that the *Ctrl* and *Enter* keys should be used together; ie, press *Ctrl*, hold it down and press *Enter*.

Jean Miles

Future Business Books
Future Publishing Ltd
Seven Dials
Saw Close
Bath BA1 1EN

Future Business Books,
Future Publishing Ltd,
Seven Sials,
Saw Close,
Bath BA1 1EN, Avon.

Second Edition January 1994

ISBN 1 85870 012 4

British Library Cataloguing in Publication Data

A CIP catalogue record for this book is available from the British Library

Commissioned and edited by Graham Douglas
Designed by P Kingett, Bath
Printed and bound by Beshara Press, Cheltenham.

CONTENTS

INTRODUCTION

Money Management with Quicken is about an accounting program which takes the hard work out of small business bookkeeping and financial management. It is also about an accounting program which greatly eases the task of domestic budgeting, giving you a complete picture of your personal finances. These are two aspects of the same software: Intuit's Quicken. Shedding its transatlantic accent and entering a competitive UK market, Quicken has rapidly established a name for ease-of-use, power and flexibility.

If you run a business, sound accounting is your life's blood; if not, you might wonder why you should bother. Who needs a personal finance program anyway? Why make yourself miserable? The answer is straightforward: if your accounts are in order, you're in charge. No matter how dire the situation, there are advantages in knowing the boundaries of the problem. Decisions, large and small, become easier. Of course, starting to get organised does take a little effort, but the results are well worth it; you can plan for the future with a real sense of direction.

Quicken 6.0 runs on industry standard IBM-compatible personal computers; requiring a hard disk, DOS 2.0 or later, with a minimum of 512KB RAM . Quicken 2.0 for Windows runs on 286 (or higher) IBM-compatible PCs with a minimum of 2MB RAM, a monitor supported by Windows and a hard disk with at least 3MB of available storage space. Quicken for Windows offers additional features, most notably in financial graphs, but is essentially the same program. It can use the same data files as Quicken 6.0.

This book was written around (DOS-based) Quicken 6.0, with illustrations (screen shots) taken from that version; the instructions showing how to move around within the program relate to Quicken 6.0 only. But all the advice about how to shape Quicken to your purposes applies equally to Quicken 2.0 for Windows. This book is intended to make a friendly program even easier to use and if you're new to computers or account-keeping, it will show you some tricks for getting the best out of Quicken.

Although much of the book is written with domestic users in mind, the special needs of business are referred to throughout the text (with chapter 9 devoted to using Quicken as a business program). This bias toward domestic usage is not because Quicken is more suited to domestic rather than business accounts; quite the contrary. It is because business people already keep accounts, and have some idea of what they want Quicken to do for them. Domestic users may be coming fresh to the whole idea, and therefore may welcome advice about how to shape Quicken into a personal tool.

Whilst not meaning to replace Quicken's own manuals, Money Management with Quicken does, of necessity, cover some of the same ground - but don't try using it as a means to avoid paying the full price for the program. Unlike many software products, Quicken is priced for real people living in the real world. It's a very good program, with very good manuals: using it is likely to make a difference in your life. Intuit deserve to be paid for their work. They also provide first-rate help at the end of a telephone line in the unlikely event of running up against a problem you can't solve. So it's in your own interest to become a registered user

Jean Miles

CHAPTER

Unwrapping the software

FEATURING

- Installation and tutorial
- Creating your file
- Moving around in Quicken
- Screen and printer settings

The purpose of this chapter is to get you from the-moment when you unwrap your new *Quicken* package to the moment when you're ready to start typing in your own financial transactions. If you're an old hand with a computer, you'll find it all very easy. You should be able to skim through or skip the first part of this chapter. But you will want to read the practical points at the end of the chapter about how to move around in *Quicken* , and about screen display, printers, and (yes) making backups.

Installation and Tutorial

Put the *Quicken* Install Disk 1 in your floppy disk drive. Change to that drive by typing 'A:' or 'B:' and pressing `[Enter]`. Type 'Install'.

Quicken will take care of the rest, asking you questions whenever a decision is needed. You will specify whether you have a colour monitor on your computer, what disk drive and directory to install in, your printer brand and model, and whether you want to be reminded of upcoming bills. You can change your mind later about almost everything. When you see the list of printers, it will look very short and almost certainly won't appear to contain the name of your printer. Press the down arrow key on the keyboard. You can scroll down through a long list of printer names until you find the one you want.

When *Quicken* finishes the installation process, it will take you back to the C: (or D:) prompt on your hard disk. There will be a message telling you to type the letter `[Q]` to start the program. From now on, whenever you switch on your computer, that's all you need to do to get *Quicken* – type `[Q]`.

When you do so for the first time, you'll find yourself at the 'Welcome to *Quicken* ' screen, with the suggestion that you might like to see an overview of *Quicken* . It's very quick: ten minutes. Unless you're a more than ordinarily impatient type, you might as well do it. But

Quicken doesn't insist. The 'Welcome to *Quicken* ' screen also allows you to choose the manual-based 'Quick Tour', which is not particularly quick – it takes an hour; or to set up your own data straight away.

When the program has finished introducing itself by way of the overview, it will leave you at the Main Menu. In the future, when you start the program, this is where you will be. This screen is the engine room for your program. You'll come back to it often. If you ever should find yourself in a tangle – in *Quicken* , that's not very likely – press the `[Esc]` key in the upper left-hand corner of your computer keyboard repeatedly until you are back at this screen.

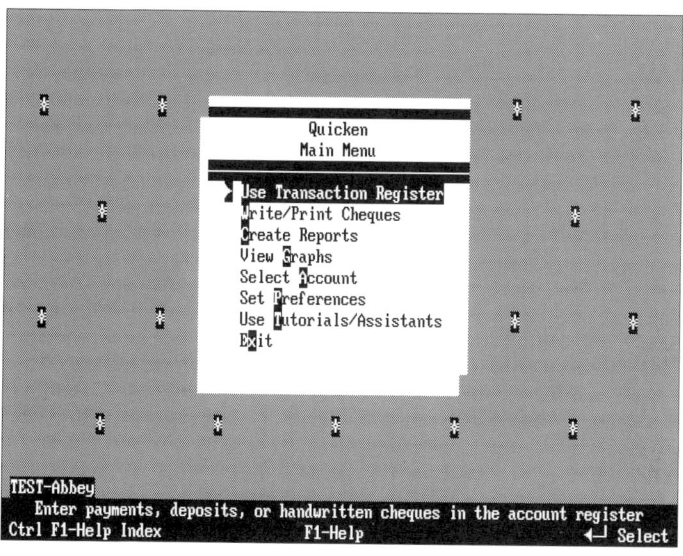

Fig. 1.1. The Main Menu

There are eight choices on the main menu. Using the arrow keys, move the highlight up and down through the choices. Notice how the line at the bottom of the screen changes, telling you the facilities offered by each choice in turn. You'll find a similarly informative line at the bottom of the screen on many other occasions when you have to make a decision of some sort.

Notice that in each of the eight choices as it is listed on the Main Menu, one letter is highlighted. You can make your choice simply by pressing the highlighted letter, or, alternatively, by moving the highlight to the item you want and pressing the `[Enter]` key. Whenever you see a list in *Quicken* with letters highlighted, all you need to do is press one of them.

Notice, too, the words at the very bottom of the screen. 'Ctrl F1 – Help Index' means that if you hold down the `[Ctrl]` key (to be found somewhere near the bottom left-hand corner of your computer keyboard) and at the same time press the `[F1]` key from the row of keys at the top of the keyboard, you will see *Quicken* 's comprehensive index of subjects you might need help with. Try it. You'll see the Help Index 'window'. Instructions for finding the topic you are interested in will also appear. Press `[Esc]` to get back to the Main Menu when you are finished exploring.

A 'window' pops up on only part of your computer screen. The rest of the screen remains visible just as it was, 'behind' the window. This book will often use the term.

Also at the bottom of the Main Menu screen you will see 'F1-Help'. Press the `[F1]` key anywhere in *Quicken* , and you will find help related to what's going on. If you press it now, you will see a Help window with information about the Main Menu itself. `[Ctrl]-[F1]` anywhere in *Quicken* will bring you the Help Index window. Remember these aids. They will smooth your path during the early days.

You will find as you work with *Quicken* that most screens contain such notes, suggesting actions you might take. If you're ever baffled, look around.

You can see the overview again, or take the quick tour, by choosing 'Use Tutorials/Assistants' from the Main Menu at any time. The quick tour is done in conjunction with a chapter in the manual, and is a very thorough introduction to the program. If you feel at all nervous about *Quicken* , perhaps because you're new to computing or to computerised accounts, take the tour.

Creating your File

From the 'Tutorials and Assistants' window, choose 'Create New File'. A 'file' in *Quicken* is a collection of accounts – current accounts, deposit accounts, perhaps a 'cash' account for the money in your pocket, credit cards; asset and liability accounts for your string of racehorses and your mortgage; share investment accounts for your stockmarket portfolio. To the file *Quicken* will add your budget categories and budget itself; and all the various things you tell the program to remember for you. A *Quicken* 'file' is made up of several DOS files. Don't worry if that sentence is meaningless to you: *Quicken* will protect you from having to think about your computer's operating system, MS-DOS, at all.

Once you have created your file and given it an appropriate name, you can start filling it with your accounts. Start with an obvious one like your current account.

From the **Main Menu**, choose '**Use Tutorials/Assistants**'

From the **Tutorials and Assistants window**, choose '**Create New Account'.**

Moving Around in Quicken

In the next chapter, you can get started typing transactions into your new account and assigning them to budget categories. Here, we are learning to move around in *Quicken.*

When you have set up your first account and provided it with an opening balance, choose the first item on the Main Menu, 'Use Transaction Register'. There you will be in the register for your new account, with the opening balance filled in as the first entry. Look at the words at the top of the screen: 'Print/Acct, Edit, Shortcuts, Reports, Activities.'

Print/Acct Edit Shortcuts Reports Activities F1-Help

DATE	CHQ NO	DESCRIPTION · MEMO · CATEGORY	PAYMENT		C	DEPOSIT		BALANCE	
		BEGINNING							
1/ 9 1992	Memo: Cat:	Opening Balance [Current]			X	2,230	00	2,230	00
2/ 9 1992	202001	Weirmouth Electricity Board Utilities:Ele→	59	97				2,170	03
2/ 9 1992	202002	Central Market Groceries	185	98				1,984	05
4/ 9 1992	SPLIT	Pay deposit Salary				2,425	00	4,409	05
5/ 9 1992		Transfer [Savings]	2,000	00				2,409	05

Current (Alt+letter accesses menu)
Esc-Main Menu Ctrl← Record Ending Balance: £873.77

Fig. 1.2. Transaction Register

That line is called the 'toolbar'. If you hold down the `[Alt]` key, probably to be found somewhere near the bottom of your computer keyboard, and at the same time press the highlighted first letter of one of the words on the toolbar, you will see a menu of further choices. You can move the highlight to the choice you want and press `[Enter]`, or select by pressing the highlighted letter in the phrase of your choice.

Many (not all) of the actions offered on the menus of the toolbar can be chosen more quickly by pressing the `[Ctrl]` key and some other key at the same time. For instance, you'll find 'Categorise/Transfer' on the Shortcuts menu, with `[Ctrl]-[C]` beside it. That particular menu item is offering you the list of income and expense categories, so that you can choose the one that relates to a transaction you have just typed in. You can choose Categorise/Transfer by

- moving the highlight down the Shortcuts menu until you reach it, and then pressing `[Enter]`;

- OR pressing [C], the highlighted letter, while the Shortcuts menu is visible on the screen;

- OR holding down the [Ctrl] key and pressing [C] at any time while you are using the transaction register, so bypassing the toolbar altogether.

In this book, when there is a quick way of doing something, it will always be suggested: 'Press [Ctrl]-[C] for the category list'. The possibility of using the toolbar menu instead will not be mentioned. That is simply a device to save time and avoid repetition. You can always use the toolbar if you prefer.

And if you have a mouse attached to your computer, you can use it to click on the toolbar. But again, this book won't keep saying so.

There are some lists in *Quicken* , such as the list of your accounts and the list of budget categories, which do not have highlighted letters. You can make a choice from such a list by moving the highlight with the arrow keys and pressing Enter when you get where you are going. You can also move through the list by pressing the initial letter of the item you are looking for. The highlight will move to the first item on the list beginning with that letter. It may or may not be the one you want. Keep on pressing the letter until you are at the right one. With a long list like budget categories which is not all visible on the screen at once, this is the best way to move.

As you use *Quicken* , you will soon build a considerable database of financial transactions, and you will often want to go back to take another look at something which is not visible on the screen. *Quicken* makes that easy:

Quicken will search the register for you. Press [Ctrl]-[S] for the 'Transaction to Find' window.

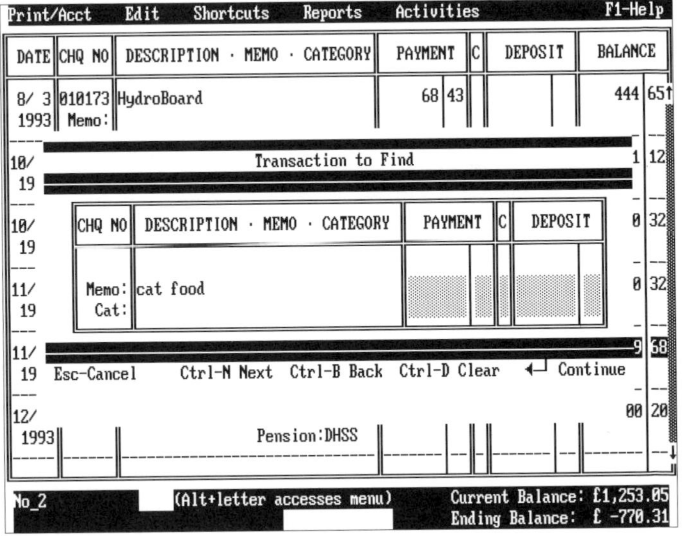

Fig. 1.3. 'Transaction to Find' window

There you can fill in anything you can remember about the transaction you are looking for – the cheque number, the payee, the amount, a memo you may have written, the category you assigned it to. Don't fill in everything. In fact, the less you put the better, as long as it identifies, or nearly identifies, the transaction you want. Then press **[Ctrl]-[B]** to search the register backwards from your present position, or **[Ctrl]-[N]** to search forwards for the next instance.

You can send *Quicken* to a particular date. From the transaction register, press **[Ctrl]-[G]**. You will see the 'Go To Date' window. Fill in the date you want, and press **[Enter]**. If the date you have entered can't be found, *Quicken* will go to the nearest date.

There are also special ways for moving about in a *Quicken* report, which may be so large that considerable portions of it exist in imaginary space surrounding your computer screen; and for moving in time when you are updating share prices. See Chapter Five for reports and Chapter Eight for stockmarket portfolios.

Screen and Printer Settings

43-line display: *Quicken* does have a tendency to spread itself out, to take a lot of space on the computer screen. Doing it that way makes things more relaxed – you will never be confronted with bewildering columns of figures you can't interpret. But occasionally you may get the feeling that you are trying to look at a landscape through a keyhole. If your computer has an EGA (Enhanced Graphics Adapter) or VGA (Video Graphics Array) monitor, help is available.

At the Main Menu, choose Set Preferences. At the Set Preferences menu, choose Screen Settings. At the Screen Settings menu, choose 'EGA/VGA 43-line display'. In the Display Mode window, choose '43 lines'. And don't worry: if you don't have the right kind of monitor for a 43-line display, *Quicken* will know about it and no harm is done.

The result is a far less elegant screen, but you will be able to see almost twice as much. Throughout this book, the illustrations show the normal *Quicken* screens, available to all users. But if you have an EGA or VGA monitor, this option is highly recommended.

Printer paper: When you installed *Quicken* , you told the program the name of your printer. But before you actually print a report, you should check the printer settings.

From the Main Menu, choose Set Preferences. From the Set Preferences menu, choose Printer Settings. Your next set of choices are these:

Settings for Printing Cheques
Settings for Printing Reports
Alternative Settings for Printing Reports

If you decide, as business users probably will, that you want *Quicken* to print your cheques, you should come back to this window later and verify the settings for cheques. For now, choose 'Settings for Printing Reports'.

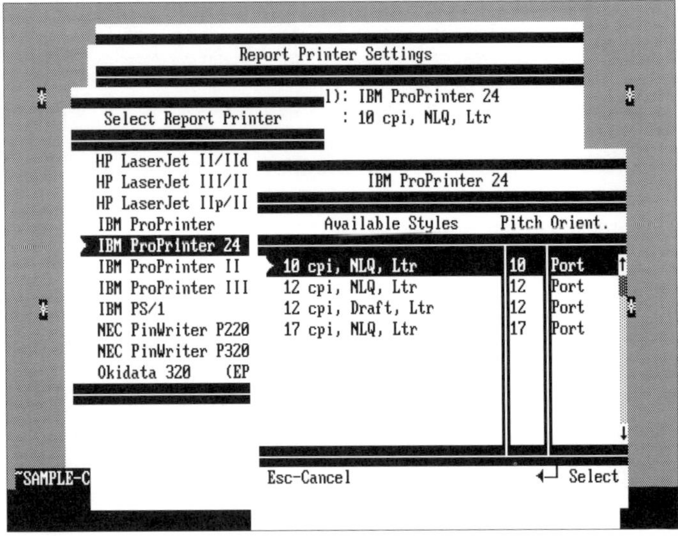

Fig. 1.4. Printer Settings

You will see a list of 'Available Styles', headed with the name of your own printer. If you have never struggled with a printer, the list may be slightly bewildering. CPI means characters per inch. (A 'character' is a letter, number, symbol or space.) In the column headed Pitch you will see the same number as has just been given for CPI. Pitch and CPI mean the same thing.

'Normal' type has 10 characters to the inch. Whatever your printer, a 10-pitch style will be available. Choose that to start with. If your printer can print smaller, you may want to come back and choose a higher pitch, probably 17 CPI, as the 'Alternative Setting for Printing Reports'. Then when you are directing a report to the printer, *Quicken* will give you the choice of which setting to use. The smaller one, like the 43-line screen, packs in more information.

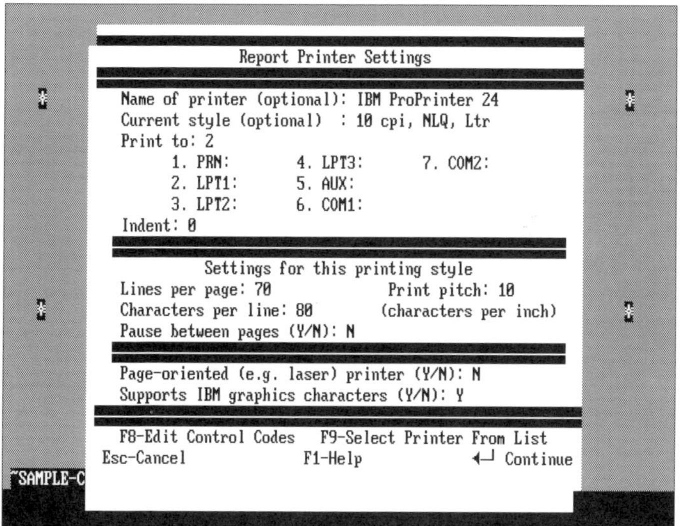

Report Printer Settings
Name of printer (optional): IBM ProPrinter 24
Current style (optional) : 10 cpi, NLQ, Ltr
Print to: 2
1. PRN: 4. LPT3: 7. COM2:
2. LPT1: 5. AUX:
3. LPT2: 6. COM1:
Indent: 0
Settings for this printing style
Lines per page: 70 Print pitch: 10
Characters per line: 80 (characters per inch)
Pause between pages (Y/N): N
Page-oriented (e.g. laser) printer (Y/N): N
Supports IBM graphics characters (Y/N): Y
F8-Edit Control Codes F9-Select Printer From List
Esc-Cancel F1-Help Continue
"SAMPLE-C

Fig. 1.5. Report Printer Settings

When you make made that choice, you will see a screen headed 'Report Printer Settings'. You may not understand some of the choices, such as the one about which 'port' to use. Don't worry: *Quicken* does understand. Just press `[Enter]` until you get to 'Lines per page.'

One of the less expected and more irritating differences between American and British life is that the standard American paper length is slightly shorter than A4 size. When you install *Quicken* , 'Lines per page' may be set to 66, the normal American length. You must change it to 70, the normal British length.

MAKING BACKUPS: Many novice users are afraid that all their records will be lost 'if I press the wrong key'. Relax: there's absolutely no danger of that happening. But don't relax so much that you begin to think you can actually trust a computer. You can't.

If you keep records on paper, you will be vulnerable to fire and flood and spilled coffee, but you are unlikely to unlock your office in the morning to discover that your ledgers have dematerialised. Computer records will vanish irretrievably in an instant if your hard disk 'goes down'. Making extra copies of your data on floppy disks and keeping those disks in a safe place doesn't take much time. *Quicken* will remind you to do it, if you like. If you establish a backup routine, it will become completely automatic. One day, you will be glad you did. Not 'may be glad' – 'will be glad'.

In Chapter Ten of this book, *Nuts and Bolts,* you will find detailed suggestions about backup techniques. Read it. And do something about it.

CHAPTER

The basics

FEATURING

- Entering a transaction
- Expense and income categories
- Cash accounts
- Credit cards
- Standing orders and direct debits

Entering a Transaction

If you're new to this sort of thing, it can all seem a bit daunting. One of the great merits of *Quicken* is that you don't have to think the whole thing out before you start. You can plunge in, see how it goes, and feel your way forward from there.

In Chapter One, you learned how to install *Quicken* and start it for the first time. As part of the process, you gave your financial data a general name and you provided the program with the details of (probably) your current account. Now it is time to start making some actual entries in that account.

● Start *Quicken* up and choose 'Use Transaction Register' from the Main Menu. There you will be with your new computerised current account, ready to start work.

● Using your cheque book stubs, and any advice slips for Switch payments you can find lying about, start to fill in transactions. The general outline of how to proceed will be familiar to you from running the *Quicken* overview (see Chapter One). It's all pretty obvious anyway.

The first column is for the date. *Quicken* will have filled it in with today's date, as set on your computer. Since you are typing in old transactions, you will have to overwrite *Quicken*'s date with the actual one for your first transaction.

The second column is headed 'Chq No' but don't worry: if you have made the payment some other way than by actually writing a cheque, you can type the word 'Switch' or 'Card' into that space, or leave it blank.

The third column is headed 'Description * Memo * Category.' None of that information is essential – *Quicken* is, mercifully, not one of those programs which puts its head down and refuses to move if you deny it some data. Normally, however, you would want to write the name of the payee on the first line. If you now press `[Enter]` you will move on to the 'Payment' column. Type the amount here, unless you are recording money paid in to your account. In that case, leave this column empty.

Another [Enter] puts you in the column headed C, for Cleared. Normally, however, you will leave that column alone. Transactions are automatically marked with an asterisk in the C column after you have cleared them while reconciling your bank statement. See Chapter Five for more on that procedure.

The next [Enter] puts you in the Deposit column. This is where you would type in an amount paid in to the account. If the transaction you are entering is something you paid out of the account, this column stays empty.

The next [Enter] puts you back in the Description * Memo * Category column, next to the word Memo. You can make a note to yourself here about just what the payment was for. You might, in the future, want to ask *Quicken* to gather together all the transactions which have the same reference on the Memo line. So keep it simple, and try to remember to include the same key word in every Memo you might later want to recall as a group. The phrase does not have to be absolutely identical every time, and you can always go back and change things later when you have a clearer idea of what you want *Quicken* to do for you.

There is one more line to fill in: the one called Category. Detailed advice follows on setting up your own budget categories. To enter a category in the transaction register, type the first few letters and press [Enter]. If it can, *Quicken* will finish the word or phrase for you. If you haven't typed enough to distinguish the category you want, the program will offer you the list and you can choose. When you find the category you are looking for, press [Enter] and *Quicken* will 'paste' it into the transaction register for you.

When you have completed the entry by filling in the Category, press [Ctrl]-[Enter] to tell *Quicken* to store the information. The program makes a pleasant little two-toned beeping sound to tell you that it has done so.

Notice at this point that the figure labelled Current Balance in the lower right-hand corner of the screen has changed to reflect the transaction you have just entered. One of the greatest advantages of taking firm hold of your accounts is that you will always know pretty accurately just how much you have in the bank. If you are fortunate enough to be in funds, you will be able to move money from a savings account into your current account just in time to save yourself from going into overdraft (and paying bank charges).

There is another figure in the lower right-hand corner as well, labelled Closing Balance. At this stage, it will probably be the same as the Current Balance. But *Quicken* lets you enter bills and receipts before the due date. If you take advantage of that useful feature, the Closing Balance will show you the amount that will be in the account when all the future events currently listed have actually happened.

Expense Categories

Quicken comes supplied with a fairly lengthy list of expense categories to start you off. Press `[Ctrl]-[C]` to have a look at it.

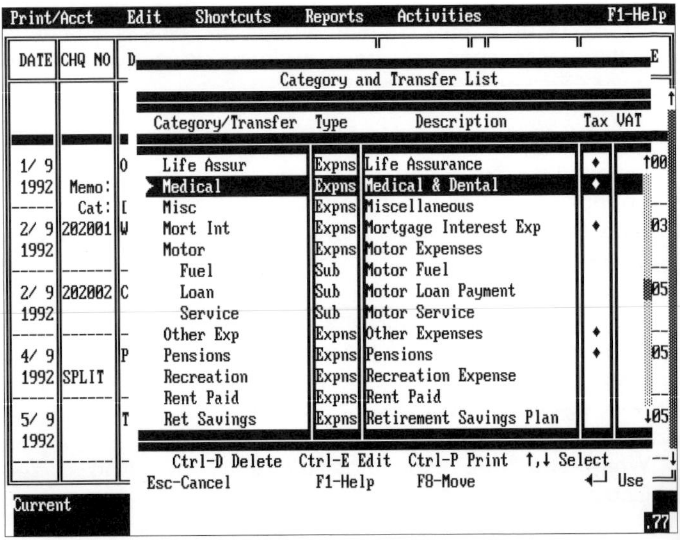

```
Print/Acct   Edit   Shortcuts   Reports   Activities              F1-Help

DATE CHQ NO  D                                                         E
                            Category and Transfer List

              Category/Transfer   Type          Description          Tax VAT

1/ 9          0  Life Assur       Expns  Life Assurance               ♦     ↑00
1992  Memo:     > Medical         Expns  Medical & Dental             ♦
      Cat:   [   Misc             Expns  Miscellaneous
2/ 9 202001  W   Mort Int         Expns  Mortgage Interest Exp        ♦      03
1992             Motor            Expns  Motor Expenses
                   Fuel           Sub    Motor Fuel
2/ 9 202002  C     Loan           Sub    Motor Loan Payment                  05
1992               Service        Sub    Motor Service
                 Other Exp        Expns  Other Expenses               ♦
4/ 9         P   Pensions         Expns  Pensions                     ♦      05
1992 SPLIT       Recreation       Expns  Recreation Expense
                 Rent Paid        Expns  Rent Paid
5/ 9         T   Ret Savings      Expns  Retirement Savings Plan            ↓05
1992
                  Ctrl-D Delete  Ctrl-E Edit  Ctrl-P Print  ↑,↓ Select
             Esc-Cancel          F1-Help      F8-Move            ←┘ Use
Current                                                                 .77
```

Fig 2.1. Category List

You can scroll down through the list with the arrow keys. As you settle in to the program, you will want to delete the categories that don't apply to you – if you live in a flat, you may not need Gardening; and if your youngest is in his mid-30s, Child Care can probably go, too. To delete a category, move the highlight to it and press `[Ctrl]-[D]`. *Quicken* will ask for confirmation before the category is deleted.

In adapting *Quicken* 's list of categories for your own use, and setting up new categories, the important thing to remember is that you can always change your mind later. Make a resolution at the beginning to think again about categories when you have been working with the program for a few weeks. Some users keep tinkering with the category list for years. Getting it right will be an important part of the process of coming to feel at home in the program.

Subcategories

Every user will have very personal views on this subject. *Quicken* is a highly relaxed and adaptable program – you're in charge here. Perhaps you want to monitor some aspects of your spending closely, and take a more unfocused view of others. Why not? You can always tighten up later on. Many people find that the best approach is to have relatively few major categories, perhaps between 12 and 15, and to make full use of *Quicken* 's subcategories. Sub-subcategories are also allowed.

As the program is supplied, the category 'Motor' provides an example of subcategories. *Quicken* offers three subcategories under Motor – Fuel, Loan, and Service. Delete Loan if you own your old banger outright – the process is just the same as for delating a main category: move the highlight to Loan and press `[Ctrl]-[D]`.

You may want to add categories for Road Tax, AA subscription, or insurance: move the highlight to the main category heading, Motor. Press `[Ctrl]-[Ins]`. You will see the Set Up Category window.

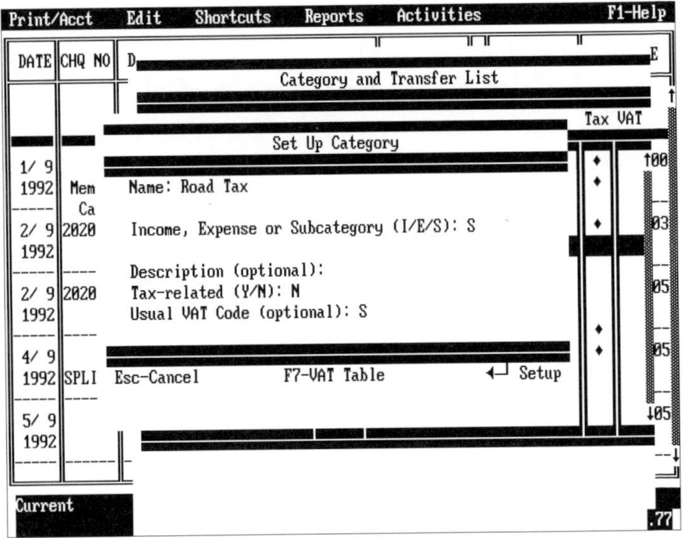

Fig 2.2. 'Set Up Category' window

The cursor will be in the Name field: type in the name of your new subcategory. That's probably all you will want or need to do. *Quicken* will already have filled in the Type of the category as 'S' (for subcategory). You could add a Description, but probably you don't need to in this case. *Quicken* asks if the category is tax-related. The answer here is No (even for Road Tax), and *Quicken* has already filled in the appropriate N. If *Quicken* 's VAT-tracking feature has been turned on, the Set Up Category window will also want to know whether transactions assigned to this category are liable to VAT, and if so what the rate is: Standard, Exempt, or Zero-Rated.

Press **[Enter]**, and your new subcategory is in place under Motor.

The great advantage of subcategories is that they can be condensed on reports so that all the expenditure is listed under the main heading – here, Motor. If you have too many main categories, it can be hard to find your way around a report; and *Quicken* does tend to spread itself on space, both on screen and on paper. On the other hand, by using subcategories you can quickly find out how much money is going on one subcategory only: what am I spending on petrol? how much does servicing cost me over a year?

As well as adding categories and subcategories of your own, you can change the name or the description of any of the categories supplied by *Quicken* . Move the highlight to the category you want to change, and press `[Ctrl]-[E]` (for Edit). You can then make any changes you like. If you have used the old category name already for some of your transactions, *Quicken* will make the change in every entry. When you come back to review categories after you have been using *Quicken* for a while, you may want to rearrange things – to move a little-used category so that it becomes a subcategory of something else; or to promote a subcategory that turns out to be a major expense in its own right. In *Quicken* , that is easy, too.

To change a category into a subcategory: From the Transac tion Register, press `[Ctrl]-[C]` as before, to see the list of categories. Move the highlight to the one you want to transform into a subcategory. Press `[F8]`. (*Quicken* does not make much use of the function keys on your computer. You may feel a bit surprised to see one of them coming into action here). You will find yourself, with your selected category, at the very top of the list.

Now move the highlight with the arrow keys, and your selected category will travel with you. Find the category under which you want to enrol it. Be careful to stop with the highlight on the name of a main category: if you stop at a subcategory, perhaps with the idea that you will show *Quicken* the exact place to put the new subcategory, you will find that you have created a sub-subcategory. That's fine, of course, if that's what you intend.

And when you have got where you were going, press `[Enter]`. *Quicken* does the rest, including making the change on any transactions already entered for the category in question.

To promote a subcategory into a main category: Press `[Ctrl]-[C]` for the list of categories. Move the highlight to the subcategory you want to promote. Press [F8]. The subcategory has now been selected for transfer, but it will stay in its place until you move it. Move the highlight to the very top of the list. Press [Enter]. The subcategory is now a main category, and you will find that *Quicken* will insert it in its proper alphabetical place in the list.

To merge two categories or subcategories: Perhaps you will find after a while that you were over-ambitious at the beginning, and that it would be simpler and more informative to merge two of your categories into one. In that case, follow the procedure above to make one of the two categories into a subcategory of the other – it makes no difference which way round you do it. If you are merging two subcategories, you will have to make one into a sub-subcategory of the other, but the procedure is exactly the same.

Then simply delete the new subcategory. (Select it and press [Ctrl]-[D].) When you delete a subcategory in *Quicken* , all its transactions are re-assigned to its main category. Your two categories are now merged. If you need a new name for the newly- merged entity, select it, press [Ctrl]-[E], and change the name and description as appropriate.

After all this, you may be surprised to learn that you do not have to assign a transaction to a category at all. Leave that line blank in the Transaction Register, and the item will turn up in your reports as 'Other'.

Obviously, you will not want to make heavy use of this feature. The whole point of entrusting your finances to *Quicken* is to find out where the money is going.'Other' is not much help towards answering that question. But 'Other' does have its uses:

- When you are reconciling a bank statement, and get to the point where the difference between the bank's figures and your own is so small that it's not worth spending any more time to track it down. *Quicken* will make an automatic adjustment in your account if you wish, and call it 'Other' (or assign it to any other category you choose).
- If you decide not to try to keep track of every single penny

you spend. Some of the outflow from your wallet will probably wind up as 'Other'.

● Most useful of all, when an item obviously belongs to a particular category but doesn't fit into any of the subcategories. For instance, you may treat your car to a wash. That is not exactly Motor:Service, you may feel. It is certainly not Motor:Fuel or Motor:Loan or Motor:Road Tax. Simply assign it to 'Motor' – it will turn up on reports as 'Motor: Other'.

Two final points:

● Life is never as simple as we would like it to be. Many *Quicken* users find they need a category with a name like 'Large Unplanned' to accommodate, well, large unplanned expenditure.

● No book can give you much advice on the problem most likely to arise as you undertake serious account-keeping. And that is, what about the money spent by your partner? There are as many possible answers to this as there are partnerships. The main thing is, take it easy. Even large, irregular entries under 'Other' are not too high a price to pay for domestic harmony.

Income Categories

Assigning income categories is not likely to take you long unless you're the Duke of Westminster. Your pay or pension, Child Benefit, a bit of interest from the building society: you will be able to adapt *Quicken* 's list easily by now. Anything which is paid regularly and automatically directly into a bank account can be set up as a Standing Order. See the section on that subject later in this chapter.

More Accounts

By this time you will have begun to get the feel of *Quicken* And you will probably realise that you are going to need to tell the program about some more of your accounts.

If you have a deposit account, a building society account, or a Post Office ordinary or investment account, add them to the list next.

From the Main Menu, choose 'Select Account'. The next

screen will show you a list of your accounts. The top item will be <New Account>. Move the highlight there and press **[Enter]**. You will find the 'Set up New Account' screen, familiar already because you used it from the Tutorial/Assistants menu to set up your current account at the beginning.

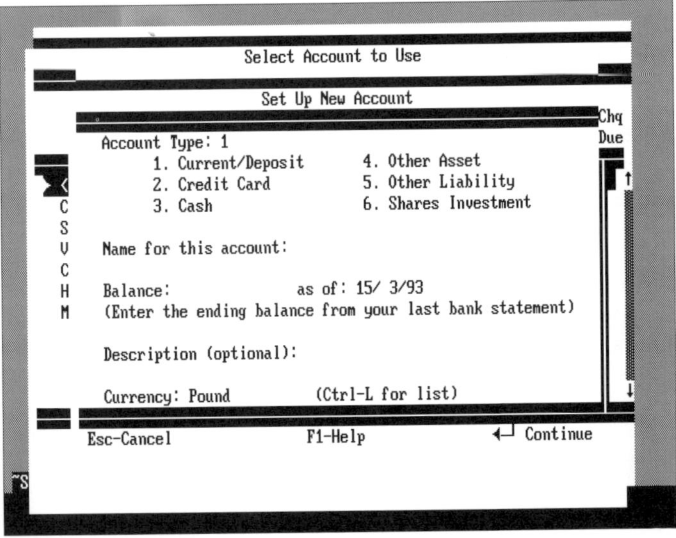
Select Account to Use

Set Up New Account

Account Type: 1
1. Current/Deposit
2. Credit Card
3. Cash
4. Other Asset
5. Other Liability
6. Shares Investment

Name for this account:

Balance: as of: 15/ 3/93
(Enter the ending balance from your last bank statement)

Description (optional):

Currency: Pound (Ctrl-L for list)

Esc-Cancel F1-Help ↵ Continue

Fig 2.3. 'Set Up New Account' window

Fill in the details. Don't worry if your passbook hasn't been brought up to date recently. Put in the latest balance you have, and its date. When your passbook is next updated, you can add the interest to the account in *Quicken* and declare it as 'Interest Income'. It doesn't matter that the date you provide for this account may be different by months from the first date you used for the current account. It is much easier to get started in *Quicken* than in most other budget programs, and one of the reasons is that *Quicken* is so easy-going about starting dates. You'll see later on how it works.

Now that you have several accounts, you may want to know how to transfer money from one to another in *Quicken* . Like everything else, it's easy. Use the Transaction Register of the account you are taking the money from. When you get to the Category line, instead of an expense or income category, put the name of the account the money is going to. When you have pressed `[Ctrl]-[Enter]` to complete the transaction, *Quicken* will put square brackets around the name of the account which receives the money. That way, as you look back through the register, it is easy to tell real transactions from the ones when you were just shifting your funds from one place to another.

Now there are some important decisions to be made. Are you going to define a cash account? and what about the credit cards?

A 'cash account' is the money in your pocket. The question is, what to tell *Quicken* about what happens to that money? The alternatives are stark black and white, but in fact there are several shades of grey available.

Cash Accounts

No cash account – You could face the fact that you would hate to have to think about *Quicken* every time you paid a bus fare or bought a newspaper. Whenever you draw cash from your current account, you could just put it down as 'Other'.

A cash account – You could set up a 'Cash' account in *Quicken* – the procedure is exactly the same as you have just gone through to set up your current and your deposit accounts. Then when you draw cash, you enter the withdrawal in *Quicken* as a transfer from your current account to your cash account.

The shades of grey

● Even if you don't have a cash account, you can enter major cash purchases in *Quicken* . Get into the habit of tucking receipts into a corner of your wallet where you can find them again. Then, when you're having a major session with *Quicken*, you can go back to the last cash withdrawal from your current account and split the transaction. The procedure for splitting is described later in this chapter: it is a very useful one, which you will rely on often. In this case, you will itemise the things you have receipts for, and assign them to their proper expense categories. Perhaps you can include a pretty good guess for regular out-of-pocket expenses such as lunches and fares to work. Then only the left-over, unexplained cash need be assigned to 'Other'.

● If you do set up a cash account, you still don't have to account for every farthing. Keep receipts and make intelligent guesses, as above, only this time you will enter them directly in the Transaction Register of the cash account. Every so often, you will want to count the money you actually have on you. You can take it for granted that you will have less than the amount *Quicken* shows as the Current Balance of your cash account – that is, some cash, perhaps quite a lot of it, will have vanished into thin air in the way money has.

At least *Quicken* will do the accounting for you: from the transaction register of your cash account, press **[Alt]-[A]** to select the Activities menu from the toolbar at the top of the screen. From the menu, select Update Account Balance.

```
Print/Acct  Edit  Shortcuts  Reports  Activities                F1-Help
DATE  REF  DESCRIPTION · MEMO · CATEGORY  SPEND      RECEIVE   BALANCE
6/ 9       Lunch                          18 50                31 50
1992                 Dining
9/
1                 Update Account Balance
10
1   Update this account's balance to   :
    Category for adjustment (optional):
22  Adjustment date               15/ 3/93
1
22 Esc-Cancel              F1-Help                  ↵ Continue
1
15/ 3
1993  Memo:
      Cat:
Cash        (Alt+letter accesses menu)
                                      Ending Balance:  £36.55
```

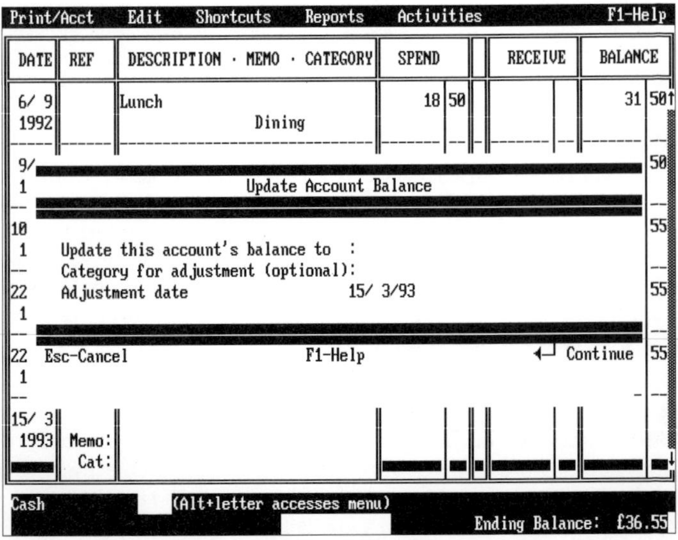

Fig 2.4 'Update Account Balance' window

You will see a form with the cursor in position for you to

type in the actual amount of money you have just discovered, by counting, that you have. You can assign the missing money to a category, perhaps 'Household'. You could even have a category called Black Hole especially for absent cash. Or you can leave that line blank, and *Quicken* will record the expense as Other. When you have finished filling in the form, press `[Enter]`, and *Quicken* will make the adjustment to the Current Balance of your cash account.

● Or you can try to keep track of every penny you spend. It's not as hard as it sounds, especially if you use your computer most days and get into the habit of starting each session with a few moments of *Quicken* . In fact, using the program is so much fun that you may find yourself nipping out for a pack of Polo Mints just to have something to enter. Even if you are trying to keep track of everything, there are bound to be times when you will have to let *Quicken* make a balance adjustment as above.

> **TIP: Even the most fanatic devotee of *Quicken* might not want to make a separate entry in the Transaction Register for each separate postage stamp or packet of fags purchased. It's easy to keep a running total for expenses like that.**

The best way is probably to keep a separate running total each month. When you buy your first stamp or magazine or pack of cigarettes of each month, enter the purchase in the cash account Transaction Register. Date it the first of the month, even if the actual purchase was made some days later – *Quicken* sorts transactions by date, no matter in what order they are entered. That way, all your running totals will be kept together.

On the first line of the Description * Memo * Category column, put something like 'Cash: cigarettes' or 'Cash:stamps and stationery'. Finish the transaction in the normal way, including assigning it to an expense category.

Then, the next time you make the same sort of purchase, use *Quicken* 's Search feature to take you back to that first-of-the-month entry. Press `[Ctrl]-[S]`. You will find a form to fill in, just like an entry in a Transaction Register. Ignoring all the rest of it, type 'Cash:' in the Description column. Then press `[Ctrl]-[B]` to search the register backwards. The highlight will stop on the first instance it finds of one of your running totals. It doesn't matter if it turns out not to be the one you are looking for. The others will be right there, because you have dated them all for the first of the month. Move the highlight to the one you want, and press `[Enter]` or the [Tab] key until the cursor is in the Spend column.

Use the *Quicken* calculator to add the new expense to the running total. There is more information on the calculator later in this chapter. `[Ctrl]-[Enter]` confirms the alternation as usual. `[Ctrl]-[End]` will take you back to the end of the Transaction Register, if you have any more spending to enter.

Print/Acct Edit Shortcuts Reports Activities F1-Help

DATE	REF	DESCRIPTION · MEMO · CATEGORY	SPEND	RECEIVE	BALANCE
1/ 1 1993	Memo: Cat:	cash:newspapers, magazines Household:papers	36 52		7 25
1/ 1 1993		cash:stamps, stationery Household:sta→	19 22		-11 97
1/ 1 1993		cash:groceries Groceries:out→	34 76		-46 73
1/ 1 1993		cash:HADM HADM	83 38		-130 11
1/ 1 1993		cash:contributions Charity	17 61		-147 72
1/ 1 1993		cash:car parks, bus fares Entertain:tra→	2 00		-149 72

cash (Alt+letter accesses menu)
Esc-Main Menu Ctrl↵ Record Ending Balance: £21.72

Fig 2.5 Running Totals in Cash Account

There is a drawback to this system. If you forget whether or not you have already added in a particular item, *Quicken* can't help. If you think that is a real danger in your case, you'd better stick to adding small items of expenditure one by one.

Credit Cards and Store Charge Cards

The choices are much the same here as for cash.

● You could just set up 'Credit Card' as an expense category and make a monthly payment to it when the bill comes in, splitting the transaction if there are any particular items on the credit card you wanted to record separately.

● Or you could set up a separate Credit Card account for each of your plastic friends, and record each transaction as soon as possible from the vouchers you carefully save.

● Or you could enter the transactions in *Quicken* from the bills when they arrive.

● Or, if you go in for credit cards in a big way, you could have a separate account or accounts for the cards you use a lot, and lump the rest together in an expense category called 'Credit Cards'.

And whichever method you choose, you can always let *Quicken* enter a balance adjustment for you, as a way of lumping together the transactions you don't want to bother to itemise separately. It is done as part of the process of checking your monthly statement – see the section *Reconciling a Statement* in Chapter Five.

Once you have set up two or three accounts and entered a few transactions, it is time to start learning some of the features that make *Quicken* so easy to use.

Splitting a transaction: There will be times when one payment (cash, cheque, Switch or credit card) will cover several items which belong in different categories. Perhaps you drew some cash with your Switch card while paying for groceries at the supermarket counter, or bought cat food, a calculator, and a couple of video tapes while you were paying for petrol. You can press `[Ctrl]-[S]` for the Split Transaction screen at any point when you are working in a Transaction Register, but the easiest thing to do is to start entering the transaction in the normal way and type

`[Ctrl]-[S]` after you have entered the total amount spent.

```
Print/Acct   Edit   Shortcuts   Reports   Activities                F1-Help
DATE  CHQ NO  DESCRIPTION · MEMO · CATEGORY  PAYMENT   C  DEPOSIT   BALANCE
3/ 3  switch  Tesco's                          81 72   X             987 08
1993  SPLIT
-----    Cat: Groceries:supermarkets
5/ 3  switch  Sainsbury's                      86 37   X             900 71
                          Split Transaction
          Category                       Memo                  Amount
 1:Groceries:supermarkets                                       31.72
 2:[cash]                                                       50.00
 3:
 4:
 5:
 6:
              Enter categories, descriptions, and amounts
Esc-Cancel    Ctrl-D Delete    F9-Recalc Transaction Total    Ctrl◄┘ Done
No_2          (Alt+letter accesses menu)    Current Balance: £1,253.05
                                            Ending Balance:  £ -770.31
```

Fig 2.6 'Split Transaction' window

On the Split Transaction screen, type in the category, a memo (if you like) and the amount for the first part of the transaction. *Quicken* immediately calculates how much is left for the other slices of the split. If you are simply dividing the transaction in two, all you have to do is type in the second category and second memo. If there are to be more fractions, type in the second sum as well, and again *Quicken* will calculate how much you have left to distribute. The program, normally so obliging about letting you do whatever you like with your own money, sensibly won't let you leave the Split Transaction screen until the parts add up to the whole.

This feature lets you be as fussy as you like about assigning expense to the proper category, while keeping the Transaction Register right with the total amount spent listed as one transaction, just as it will be on your bank or credit card statement.

Standing Orders and Direct Debits

From the Transaction Register of any account, press [Alt]-[S] for the Shortcuts menu on the toolbar at the top of your screen, and choose Standing Orders from that menu. You will see a list of your standing orders, if you have any, with <Set up new order> at the top of the list. Choose that, and you will see the Set Up Standing Order window.

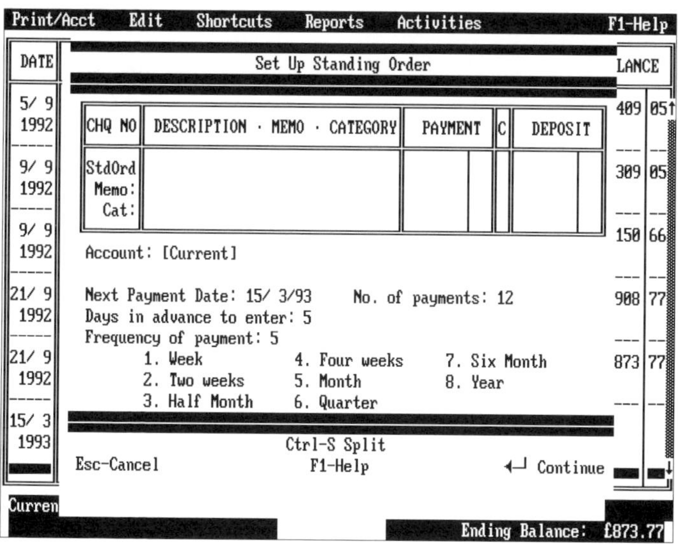

Fig 2.7 'Set Up Standing Order' window

Filling in the top part is just like making an entry in a Transaction Register. You fill in the payee, a memo, a category and the amount. For a Direct Debit – which may, unlike a Standing Order, vary in amount from time to time – you can either leave the Payment column blank or fill in an average amount. In either case you will need to come back and amend the entry each time a payment is actually made, when you know precisely how much your creditor took. For a Standing Order you can fill in the precise amount from the beginning.

In the lower half of the Set Up Standing Order form you specify which of your accounts will make the payment and when the next payment is due. The next question is

'No. of payments'. If there is an answer, fill it in; if the Standing Order or Direct Debit is of the more common until-further-notice sort, you will have to delete the answer '12' which *Quicken* has helpfully suggested for you and leave that space blank.

Next, *Quicken* asks how many days in advance the payment should be entered in the Transaction Register of your account. The program suggests the answer '5'. When *Quicken* enters a transaction in advance, it appears at the bottom of the register, of course – because its date is still in the future and therefore obviously later than the dates of the other entries which have already been paid out – below a double-ruled line, with the future date in pale, ghostly lettering.

The first time you use the program after the due date, you will see that the entry has moved above the double line and that the style of lettering has changed to match that of all the other entries.

Standing orders can be used for payments you receive and well as those you pay. It can be very comforting as your financial month staggers towards the wire to see the ghostly presence of your pay announced five days in advance. Of course you can have more or less than five days warning if you prefer – or none at all.

Finally, you must tell *Quicken* how often the payment is to be made or credited. The range of options here is excellent. As well as 'week', 'month', 'quarter' and 'year', which might be expected, *Quicken* also offers 'two weeks', 'half month', 'four weeks' and 'six month'. When you leave this screen to return to the Transaction Register, don't worry if the Standing Order you have just entered doesn't appear to be there, even though it is due. It will be there the next time you use *Quicken* .

Memorised Transactions

You probably find that the names of some payees turn up again and again. If you like, you can memorise such transactions and let *Quicken* fill them in for you.

When you have entered a transaction you want to memorise, perhaps a cheque to the supermarket or the gas board, type it into the Transaction Register as usual, and then press [Ctrl]-[M]. *Quicken* will highlight the information and ask for confirmation that you want it memorised. You can leave the amount out, or put it in and change it next time.

To recall the memorised transaction, press [Ctrl]-[T] from the Transaction Register. You will see a list of the memorised transactions. Move the highlight to choose the one you want, and press [Enter].

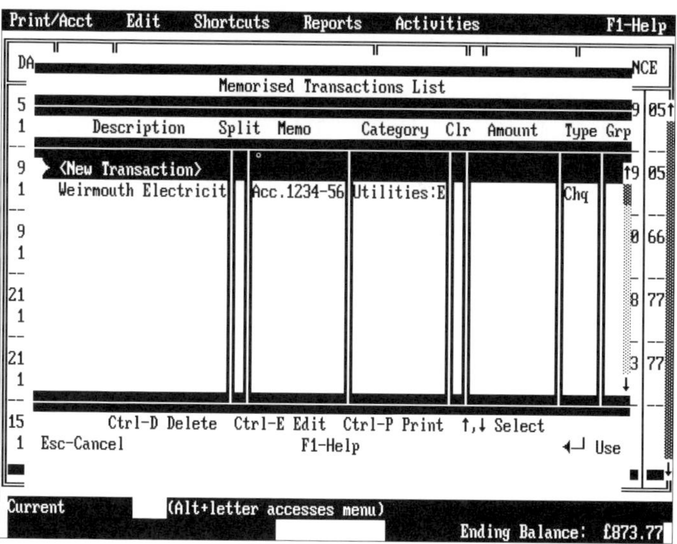

Fig 2.8 Memorised Transactions List

Then you can change any details which need changing, such as the amount. To change a memorised transaction permanently, highlight it on the list and press [Ctrl]-[E] for Edit.

The *Quicken* calculator

From anywhere in the program, even the Main Menu, [Ctrl]-[O] (the letter 'O', not the number '0') produces a neat little calculator on the left-hand side of the screen. Type in a number. Then type a mathematical sign, [+], [-],

[*], or [/] – they are called 'operators'. The [*] is the sign of multiplication on a computer, as you probably already know, and [/] means 'divided by'. Type in another number. Type [=] or press [Enter]. And there's your answer. It's better than a real calculator, because the numbers that made up the sum are still visible on what *Quicken* calls the 'paper' above the display where you have been typing. If you want to do a further calculation using the answer to your previous sum, just carry on: type another operator, then another number.

While you are using the calculator, typing [C] clears away all numbers. [Esc] gets rid of the calculator.

You can also calculate percentages without having to remember what you learned at school about how to do it. To find (let us say) 7.65% of 832,

simply type 7.65%

then ....*

then 832

and press .... [=] **or** [Enter].

To add 8.3% of £832 to the original amount,

type £832

then ....+

then 8.3%

and press .... [=] **or** [Enter].
Easy.

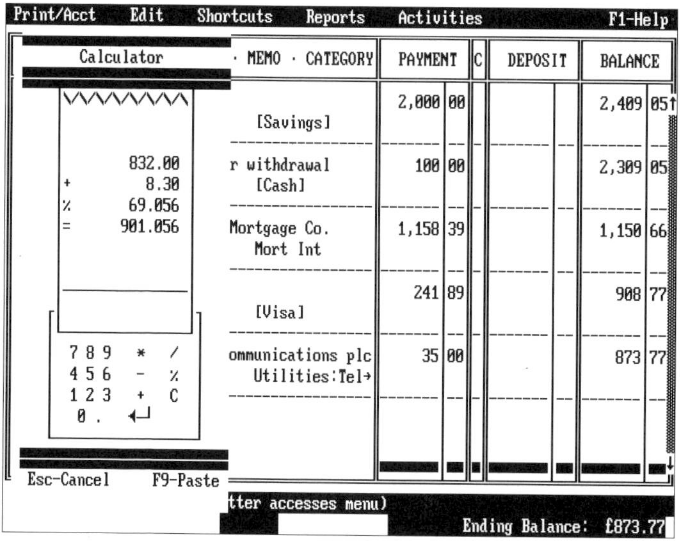

```
Print/Acct   Edit   Shortcuts   Reports   Activities                    F1-Help

   Calculator          · MEMO · CATEGORY  PAYMENT   C  DEPOSIT   BALANCE
                                          2,000 00              2,409 05
                         [Savings]
          832.00       r withdrawal         100 00              2,309 05
 +          8.30         [Cash]
 %         69.056
 =        901.056      Mortgage Co.       1,158 39              1,150 66
                         Mort Int
                                            241 89                908 77
                         [Visa]
  7 8 9   *   /        ommunications plc     35 00                873 77
  4 5 6   -   %          Utilities:Tel→
  1 2 3   +   C
   0 .   ←┘

 Esc-Cancel    F9-Paste
                       tter accesses menu)
                                          Ending Balance:  £873.77
```

Fig 2.9 The Quicken Calculator

Better yet: if you use the calculator when your cursor is positioned in one of the columns of a Transaction Register which contains a number, the calculator lifts that number into its display, ready for you to add or subtract or calculate 8.3%. When you're finished, if you want the result of your calculations to replace the number in the Transaction Register, press **[F9]** to paste it in. Otherwise press **[Esc]**, as usual, to get out of the calculator. You will still have to press **[Ctrl]-[Enter]** to confirm to *Quicken* that you want the program to replace the old transaction with one containing the new amount.

If you decide you have made a horrible mistake, and realise to your dismay that you can't remember what the number in the Transaction Register was before you started playing with the calculator, just use the arrow keys to move the cursor away from that entry in the Register. *Quicken* won't let you go without asking whether you want to record or to abandon the change you have just made. And if you choose the answer 'Cancel changes and leave', everything will be all right again.

Classes: A Real Gem

There is one more subject you ought to know about as part of the process of getting started in *Quicken* . That is, Classes. When you are working on reports (see Chapter Four), you will notice that 'Classes' are often listed as one of the possible ways to group or to subtotal transactions. You may never need or want to use this facility.

But if you do want them, Classes provide an easy way of grouping together items of expenditure which occur in different categories. You could accomplish the same thing by careful use of the Memo field, but if you know you want to group transactions in this way, using Classes is safer because *Quicken* will jog your elbow, if need be, to specify the same Class each time, not just a vaguely similar word.

How do you assign a transaction to a Class? Easy, as usual. When you have typed the category or subcategory for the transaction, type a forward slash, [/], and then the name of a Class. (Leave the category out if you like, but do include the forward slash to tell *Quicken* that the name of a Class is to follow.)

Quicken does not come with a list of Classes, as it does with Categories. You're completely free here to invent whatever Classes you like. The first time you enter the name of a Class, *Quicken* will tell you that it does not know of that Class and ask whether you want to add it to the list. And so it goes: if you type in the name of a Class already on the list, *Quicken* accepts it without question. If it is new (or if you have spelled it wrong: *Quicken* can't tell the difference) the program will ask you to verify that you want it added to the list of Classes. If you prefer, you can view the current list and select the one you meant. You can also add new Class names directly to the list, just as you did with category names. From the Shortcuts menu on the toolbar, choose Select/Set Up Class.

You can even have subclasses.

And what is the point of all this? The main users of Classes will probably be those who run business enterprises intertwined with domestic finances: a Bed and Breakfast business, for example; a consultancy run from home; the letting of your converted farmhouse in the Dordogne during the months when your family aren't in residence there. For tax purposes, you want to keep track of transactions which relate specifically to the business; but you don't want to keep a separate bank account for the purpose.

As you become familiar with *Quicken* , you will probably think of ways to use Classes for yourself if your finances are of the sort which need additional classification. See Chapter Eight, on *Quicken* 's role as your financial adviser; and Chapter Nine, on the business uses of *Quicken*, for further suggestions. And if ever you find yourself tearing your hair because you want *Quicken* to do something specific for you, and can't work out how to persuade the program to cooperate, think of Classes before you despair.

CHAPTER

Budgeting with Quicken

FEATURING

- First - time budgeting
- Automatic budgeting
- Using averages
- Saving and retrieving budgets

So far, you have learned how to set up accounts, expense categories, and income categories; how to enter transactions in *Quicken*; how to transfer money between accounts. *Quicken* has already made itself useful by telling you the balance in your current account, and the Closing Balance as well if you have made entries in advance of today's date. And *Quicken* has been set up to deal with your Standing Orders and Direct Debits, adding in your pay when the happy day comes round, and removing the money for the mortgage when it's time to do that.

First - Time Budgeting

If you're going to get the best out of the program, the next thing you ought to think about is setting a budget for yourself. Estimate how much you are likely to spend each month – you're bound to be wrong, at first. And then monitor your actual spending against the estimates, improving the estimates as you go along. As you will see, this tedious job has to be done only once. Later on, you will use your actual accounts to budget for the future.

From the Transaction Register of any of your accounts, press `[Alt]-[A]` to select the Activities menu from the toolbar. Then select 'Set up Budgets' from that menu. You will find a screen with your income (above) and expense categories down the left hand side, and columns of zeros headed with the names of the months filling most of the rest of the screen. There isn't room for all 12 months on the screen – but they are 'there', off to the right, and you can move the cursor to them. Setting up a budget involves typing in estimated expenses to replace the zeros.

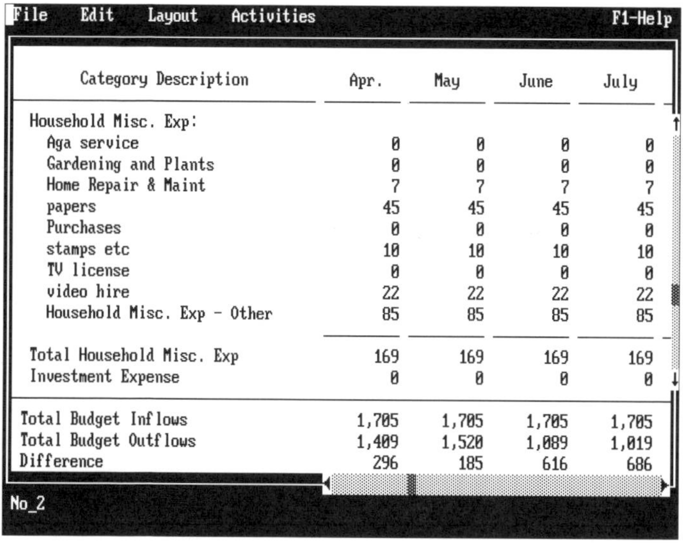

File Edit Layout Activities F1-Help

Category Description	Apr.	May	June	July
Household Misc. Exp:				
Aga service	0	0	0	0
Gardening and Plants	0	0	0	0
Home Repair & Maint	7	7	7	7
papers	45	45	45	45
Purchases	0	0	0	0
stamps etc	10	10	10	10
TV license	0	0	0	0
video hire	22	22	22	22
Household Misc. Exp - Other	85	85	85	85
Total Household Misc. Exp	169	169	169	169
Investment Expense	0	0	0	0
Total Budget Inflows	1,705	1,705	1,705	1,705
Total Budget Outflows	1,409	1,520	1,089	1,019
Difference	296	185	616	686

No_2

Fig. 3.1. The Budget Screen

If you prefer, you can budget by the quarter or even by the year. Press `[Alt]-[L]` for the Layout menu from the toolbox at the top, and make the appropriate selection. Most of us find it easier to do it month by month.

You can suppress your subcategories (and sub- subcategories) if you like, or have them visible.

Press `[Alt]-[E]` for the Edit menu and choose 'Subcats'. If you assign budget amounts to a subcategory and then decide to suppress them for a while, *Quicken* will lump in the budgeted amount with the top category – the one the subcategories live under. But the program will remember the amounts you assigned to the subcategories, and you can view the more detailed budget again whenever you choose. Begin with the easy categories. Most of your income, probably, and some of your outgoings are likely to be the same every month. The mortgage, for example; your pay, if it doesn't fluctuate with bonuses or overtime (and you might consider putting those in separate income categories if it does); Child Benefit; any payments you have arranged to make in monthly instalments for major bills such as gas or electricity or insurance premiums; television rental. Your bank statement should serve to jog your memory about regular incomings and outgoings.

Next, estimate – the more accurate word might be guess – a sum for categories such as Food, Household, Petrol and Leisure on which you spend money fairly constantly. You may need to guess at some of the income categories, too. You will have to revise your early guesses – probably upward for expense and downward for income – when you have been keeping accurate figures for a few months. But try.

Quicken is, as often, ready to do some of the hard work for you. When you have filled in January with the constant amounts and the guesses at other regular receipts and payments, press `[Alt]-[E]` for the Edit Menu and choose Fill Columns. *Quicken* will copy the amounts you have entered into the other 11 months. If you prefer, you can do this category by category: position the cursor on the amount you want to copy; press `[Alt]-[E]` for the Edit Menu; and choose Fill Right. *Quicken* will copy the amount under your cursor to the months to the right.

The next thing to do is to gather together all the evidence you can find for the bills which don't occur monthly but whose arrival can be accurately predicted: gas, electricity and telephone, assuming you don't have Direct Debit arrangements with the companies to make a monthly payment; Council Tax, likewise; water rates; Road Tax; insurance bills. Then there are bills which are certain and fairly regular, but don't have an easily predictable date: car servicing, heating oil. Use old bills to estimate for the future. Bear in mind, of course, that fuel bills like electricity and gas will be heavier in the winter; whereas other bills, such as the telephone, ought to be unrelated to the season.

You are certain to forget some items, no matter how hard you try at this stage. Whenever you find yourself paying a bill which you realise you haven't budgeted for, come back to this screen and add a budget amount so that it won't catch you out next time.

Notice at the bottom of the screen the useful line which

shows, for each of the visible months, Total Budget Inflows, Total Budget Outflows, and Difference. It can be predicted with fair assurance that you will go over budget often: try to ensure, therefore, that you have a 'cushion' budgeted for most months.

Automatic Budgeting

How? just keep accounts for a while, and then let *Quicken* use your actual spending to predict the future.

To use that feature realistically, you should really keep records for three months at least. But you will probably want to try it out after only one month, and there's no harm in doing so. From the Budget screen, press `[Alt]-[E]` for the Edit menu of the toolbar. Choose AutoCreate. The 'Automatically Create Budget' screen then invites you to specify the date range to copy from, and the months to copy to.

```
File    Edit    Layout    Activities                              F1-Help

     Category Description           Jan.      Feb.      Mar.      Apr.

   Electricity                         0         0         0         0
   Gas                                                     0         0
   Telephone          Automatically Create Budget          0         0
   Domestic Bills                                          0         0
                   Copy from:  1/92 through: 12/92
 Total Domestic B  Place budget starting in month: 1       0       140
 Entertainment:    Round values to nearest: 1
   fares, car par        1. £1          3. £100            5         5
   tickets               2. £10                           45        45
   travel          Use average for period (Y/N): N        50        50
   Entertainment                                          25        25
                  Esc-Cancel     F1-Help     ◄┘ Continue
 Total Entertainm                                        125       125

 Total Budget Inflows            1,760     1,760     1,760        50
 Total Budget Outflows           1,554     1,019     1,019     1,159
 Difference                        206       741       741    -1,109
Abbey
```

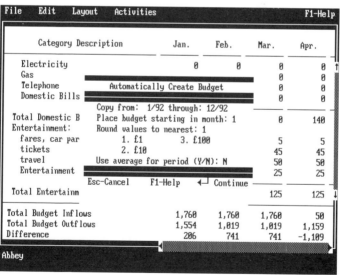

Fig. 3.2. Automatic Budgeting

Months are specified by number: January is 1 and so forth in the usual way.

Using Averages

The same menu choice, AutoCreate, can be used to ask *Quicken* to take an average of your expenditure, going as far back as you like and as far as you have data to offer, and copy the averages into whatever month you specify. If you are budgeting by quarter instead of by month, AutoCreate can use your data about the past to create averages for a quarter – and that approach will be more accurate, if you have major quarterly bills.

The one drawback to *Quicken*'s helpfulness here is that there is no way to combine these methods. AutoCreate will either copy your actual data to create future budgets, or take an average of it. But there are categories for which averages are best – food, petrol, clothes; and others where actual bills would provide a better basis – Council Tax, TV licence, insurance premiums. *Quicken* won't do averages category- by-category. It's all or nothing.

If you're in any doubt which system is best for you, let AutoCreate copy actual figures. Then look up your actual total expenditure for the period in question in the categories you would rather use averages for. Do that by creating an Itemised Category report filtered so that it only shows those categories – Chapter Four tells you in detail how to do so.

When you know the totals, use the *Quicken* calculator to work out the average for yourself, dividing the overall total by the number of months (or quarters) covered by the data. Then go back to the budget screen and fill in your averages by hand in the first relevant column – it will be January, if you're budgeting for a whole year by months; Qtr. 1, if you're budgeting for a year by quarters; or whatever month or quarter you choose, if you are budgeting for only part of a year. Then use the Fill Right option from the Edit menu to copy your average to the other columns to the right.

If you have set up an expense category called Large Unplanned, as suggested in the last chapter, you might like to try this system on it. Find out how much you spent last year under that heading. Figures for less than a year are not likely to be much use here. Divide that amount by 12 and use the answer as your monthly budget for Large Unplanned for the current year. Every so often, call up a budget report for all of the current year to date (not a monthly budget report) and see how you're doing. This may take the sting out of Large Unplanneds.

The next chapter, on reports, will show you how to create budget reports and so make use of the hard work you have just done. You will be able to see exactly how your actual spending measures up to expectations. But budgets can be useful in other ways, too.

Saving and Retrieving Budgets

Quicken can only hold one annual budget at a time, although, as you will see, it can keep data files stretching as far back in time as you like. This can be slightly awkward, if you want to compare your actual spending with your current budget as you go along and, at the same time, prepare a budget for next year.

This is not a particularly serious problem, however, and there are several possible ways to work around it.

- Set up a budget as already described, and keep accounts for a year. You will want to adjust some budget items as you proceed, particularly for the regular out-of-pocket expenses such as petrol or food, whose actual totals may surprise you. Other budgetings you may want to leave unchanged, even when reality turns out to be different from expectation, as an interesting record.

- At the end of the year, print out a budget report to keep. See Chapter Four for help with constructing and printing reports. Then save your budget to disk: from the Budget screen, press `[Alt]-[F]` for the File menu. Choose 'Export Budget'.

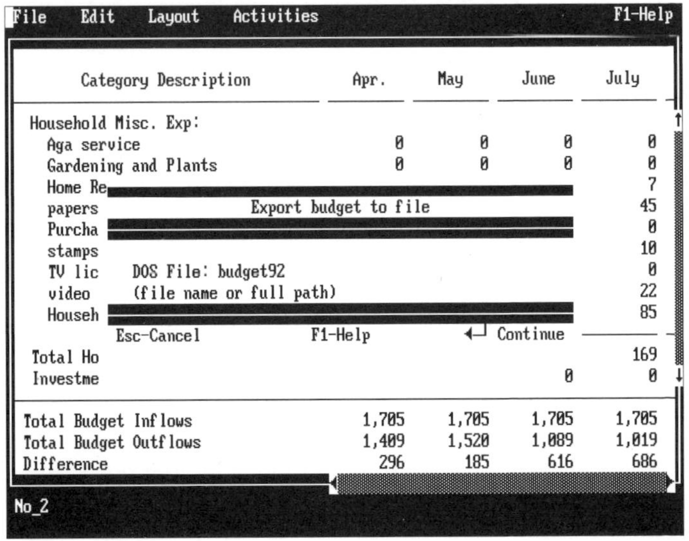
File Edit Layout Activities F1-Help

Category Description	Apr.	May	June	July
Household Misc. Exp:				
Aga service	0	0	0	0
Gardening and Plants	0	0	0	0
Home Re				7
papers				45
Purcha				0
stamps				10
TV lic				0
video				22
Househ				85
Total Ho				169
Investme			0	0
Total Budget Inflows	1,705	1,705	1,705	1,705
Total Budget Outflows	1,409	1,520	1,089	1,019
Difference	296	185	616	686

Export budget to file

DOS File: budget92
(file name or full path)

Esc-Cancel F1-Help ← Continue

No_2

Fig. 3.3. Saving a Budget

You will be asked to give the budget a file name. Choose a name that will remind you of the date, something like BUDGET92. *Quicken* will then copy all your budgeted amounts, with the corresponding categories, to a disk file.

● To get BUDGET92 back at any time in the future, choose the File menu from the toolbar again, and this time select 'Import Budget'. You will need to remember the name you have given to your stored budget, as *Quicken* does not, on this occasion, offer you a list to choose from. Your old figures will reappear, overwriting the current ones. Note, however, that this save-and-recover process for budgets will only work if the categories stay exactly the same. So don't try it if you are still tinkering with your categories.

● When the old budget is safely printed out and saved to disk, use AutoCreate from the Edit menu to make all of your actual expenditure for the past year into the budget figures for next year.

● Before you start tinkering with your newly-created budget – which equals in fact your income and expenditure for last year, category by category and month by month – save it at once under some such title as ACTUAL93. You may then want to go through and make adjustments, and to replace some of the figures with the average amounts in the way just described.

● It is interesting, occasionally, to compare current spending with last year's. Simply save your current budget – call it CURRENT; recall ACTUAL93; set up a Monthly Budget Report (see the next chapter) and browse through it. When you are finished, recall CURRENT to its place as your active budget.

Come back to the budget screen from time and look at the months ahead. Bills are irregular, especially if you don't have arrangements in place to even some of them out through the year – and many people still don't like the idea of signing a Direct Debit in favour of the gas board or British Telecom. Peering ahead at your budget will let you see a bad month coming before it arrives. Just look at those lines at the bottom of the screen: Total Budget Inflows/Total Budget Outflows/Difference. If the difference for any month is a negative figure, you'll know that it would be a good idea to put something aside in advance. The longer you work with *Quicken* the more useful your data, and your budgets, become.

CHAPTER

Reports and graphs

FEATURING

- A guided tour
- A cashflow report
- Viewing a report
- Types of graph

By now you have put lots of information into *Quicken*. But you haven't had anything much back from the program, except an up-to-date balance for your current account. Learning to get the best out of *Quicken*'s report options is one of the most important aspects of learning the program. *Quicken* has a lot of report formats, and there is a good deal you can do yourself to shape reports into the exactly the form you find most useful. It is not the easiest budget program in the world to get information out of, precisely because you have so much choice. This is the one part of the program where you will have to face up to a learning curve.

Take heart: in practice, it is not as bad as it may sound if you read this chapter away from your computer. At every step, the *Quicken* screen makes it clear what you should do or what your choices are. If you do get into a mess, just press `[Esc]` repeatedly until you are back on familiar ground. And once you have figured out what you want *Quicken* to tell you, and how to make it do so, you can have the program memorise your report format so that in the future things really will be fast and easy.

A Guided Tour

We'll start with a tour. From the Main Menu, choose Create Reports. The next menu looks like this:

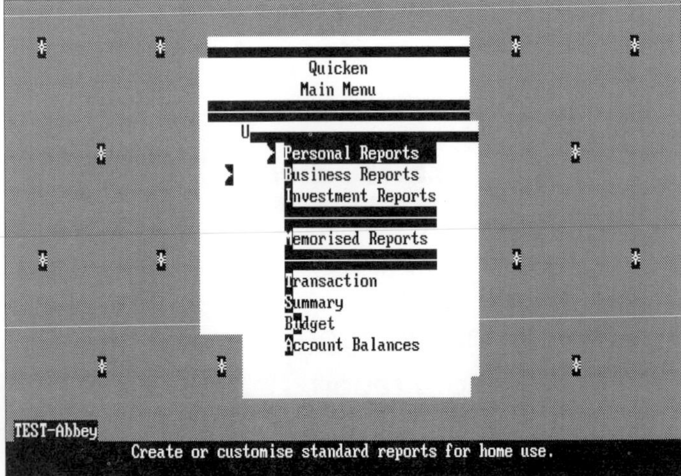

Fig. 4.1. Reports Menu

Working down the list: If you choose Personal Reports, you'll get another menu. We'll come back to that in a moment.

Business Reports are covered in Chapter Nine, on the business uses of *Quicken*.

Investment Reports are in Chapter Seven, on using *Quicken* to monitor your stockmarket investments.

Memorised Reports are the ones you will soon be saving for your own future use.

The remaining four choices are the four basic reports which *Quicken* offers. All the other Personal and Business reports are *Quicken*'s own variations on one of these four themes. And you have a lot of scope for working out variations of your own.

● A Transaction Report lists actual transactions. They can be sorted and sub-totalled in a number of different ways.

● A Summary Report summarises transactions by category and subcategory. Although individual transactions are not shown, you can zoom in on any figure in the report and get a list of the individual transactions 'behind' it.

● A Budget Report compares actual expenditure with budgeted amounts.

● An Account Balances Report lists the totals and balances for all your accounts. If you like, you can include Asset Accounts in *Quicken* to cover things like your house and furniture – more about that in Chapter Six. If you do that, an Account Balances Report will give you a picture of your net worth.

Let's go back to the top of the Menu and choose Personal Reports to get the feel of how all this actually works.
The next menu offers:

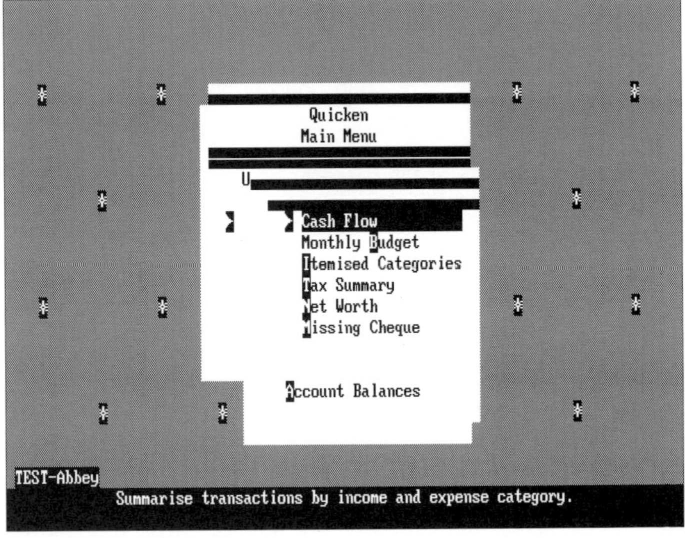

Fig. 4.2. Personal Reports Menu

We will have a look at each of these reports in turn. While exploring the first of them, Cash Flow, we will see

- how to condense and expand the information *Quicken* is presenting;
- how to filter the information; and
- how to memorise a report for future use once you have it the way you want it.

Once we know all that, we can skim more rapidly through the other types of report. Many of the techniques discussed here will be useful when you are preparing graphs, too.

A Cash Flow Report

An important concept, and a good place to start. Essentially, the idea is to compare money coming in with money going out, to see which amount is the greater. A Cash Flow Report is a variation on the Summary Report from *Quicken*'s basic list.

Choose Cash Flow from the Personal Reports menu, and you will see a screen which will become very familiar as you work with reports.

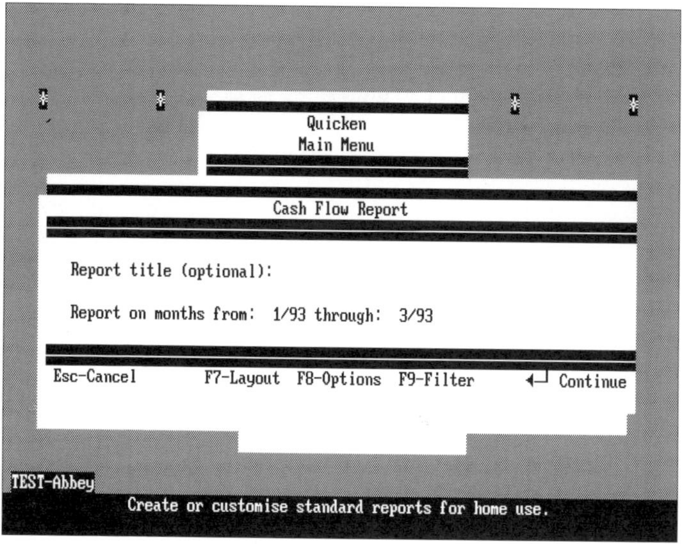

Fig. 4.3. Creating a Report

First you will be asked to give your report a title. That is not essential unless you later want to memorise the report.

Next you will be asked for the date range your report should cover. You are asked for a starting month and starting year, and a closing month and closing year. *Quicken* will already have filled in its own suggestion: that you use all the data available for the current calendar year. It's only a suggestion.

If you move the cursor to the dates *Quicken* suggests and press `[+]` or `[-]`, the dates will change, forwards or backwards, a month at a time. Or you can type in the dates you prefer. To get a report covering one month only, give the same month for both the 'from' and the 'to' date. Reports needn't cover whole months – they can start and end any time, on days you specify. We will see how to do that in a moment.

Now it is clear why there was no fuss about a starting date when you were setting up your accounts. So the credit cards and the current account all have different starting dates, and the first week of cash accounting involved a huge dump to 'Other' just to get things straight. Never mind: pick a starting date for your report when you know everything was running smoothly.

And that is all you absolutely need to do. The rest is optional. Let's have a look at the Cash Flow report now, and then come back and explore the possibilities at the bottom of the form.

Press `[Enter]` until the form goes away. You will have to wait for a moment while *Quicken* organises your data. Then you will see your Cash Flow report: income first (*Quicken* calls it INFLOWS), then expense (OUTFLOWS); finally the difference between the two. You see why they call it the bottom line: if the final figure is negative, you have spent more than you got during the period in question. If it's positive, you're OK.

```
File/Print    Edit    Layout    Reports    Activities                F1-Help

                         CASH FLOW REPORT

                    1/ 1/93 Through 31/ 3/93
JEANMILE-Bank,Cash,CC Accounts
21/ 3/93
                                                   1/ 1/93-
            Category Description                  31/ 3/93

        Motor Fuel                                   63.84
        Motor Expenses - Other                        6.00

      Total Motor Expenses                                    69.84
      Taxes                                                   26.98
      TO stock market                                        323.40

  TOTAL OUTFLOWS                                           5,861.00

  OVERALL TOTAL                                             -396.30

No_2
Esc-Leave report
```

Fig. 4.4. Part of a Cash Flow Report

Viewing a Report

Before we go on to some of the fancier things you can do with a report, here are two important techniques which you will want to use often. They work in other reports as well as the Cash Flow.

1) **On-screen display:** *Quicken* doesn't show very much of a report on screen at one time. If your computer monitor is capable of a 43-line display, you will want to choose it for reports even if you don't like it for everyday work. For how to do that, see the section at the end of Chapter One.

2) **Fast keys:** Even with a 43-line display, a report may not fit entirely on your computer screen. You can move through a report using the up arrow and down arrow keys to move one line, or `[PgUp]` (Page Up) and `[PgDn]` (Page Down) keys to move one screen. Other possible movements:

Right one column.................. `[Tab]` or right arrow
Left one column.................... `[Shift]-[Tab]` or left arrow
Right one screen.................. `[Ctrl]`-right arrow
Left one screen..................... `[Ctrl]`-left arrow

3) **Expanding the data:** Move the cursor back up to any figure in the report and press `[Ctrl]-[Z]`. After another brief pause, you will see a list of the separate transactions which made up that figure.

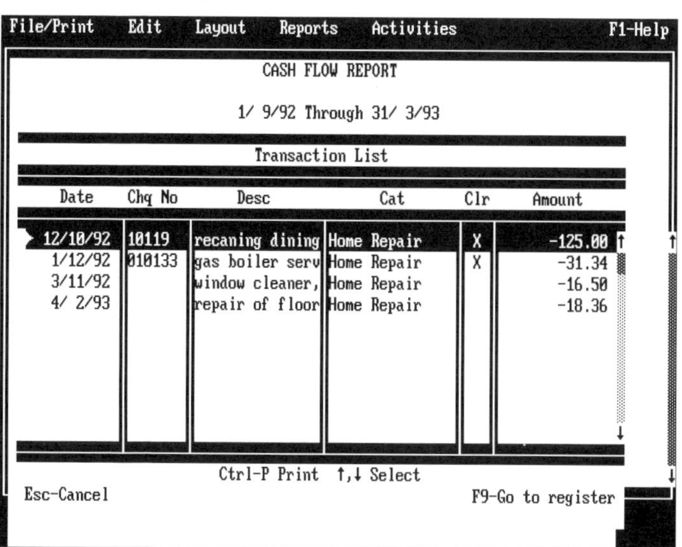

Fig. 4.5. 'Home Repair' Category Expanded

In the illustration, a 'Home Repair and Maintenance' category in a Cash Flow report has been expanded into its separate transactions.

4) **Contracting the data:** Move the cursor to one of the income or expense categories listed on the left-hand side of the screen. For this first experiment, pick one with no subcategories. Press `[-]` (the minus sign). The category disappears. You will see that a new category has been added at the end of the list, 'Inflows – collapsed' or 'Outflows – collapsed' depending on whether it was an income or an expense category you zapped. The amount belonging to the vanished category has been assigned to the new 'collapsed' category. Try another, and see how the amount in 'Inflows – collapsed' or 'Outflows – collapsed' increases to include the sum for the category no longer shown, so that TOTAL INFLOWS and TOTAL OUTFLOWS remain the same.

```
File/Print   Edit   Layout   Reports   Activities                    F1-Help

                              CASH FLOW REPORT

                          1/ 1/93 Through 31/ 3/93
  JEANMILE-Bank,Cash,CC Accounts
  21/ 3/93
                                                     1/ 1/93-
          Category Description                      31/ 3/93
  ____________________________________  ______________________________

    TOTAL JMM                                                   60.92
    memberships                                                 36.00
    Taxes                                                       26.98
    TO stock market                                            323.40
    Outflows - Collapsed                                       362.34
                                                          ___________
  TOTAL OUTFLOWS                                             5,861.00

                                                          ___________
  OVERALL TOTAL                                               -396.30
                                                          ===========

No_2
Esc-Leave report
```

Fig. 4.6. Collapsed Categories in a Report

Next, try a category that does have subcategories. Position the highlight on the 'parent' category and press the minus sign. This time, the subcategories (and sub-subcategories, if there were any) disappear, and the parent category is renamed 'Total Household', or whatever is appropriate, and shows the total expense for the group of subcategories beneath.

Now move the cursor to the line that says TOTAL OUTFLOWS, and press the minus sign again. All the categories disappear. The TOTAL OUTFLOWS line says it all.

In each case, pressing the plus sign restores the categories.

This easy way to get rid of detail lets you get a view of the whole situation, and to see the wood, so to speak, before you start inspecting the individual trees.

Now let's go back and look again at the form you filled out before you saw your Cash Flow Report. (Fig. 4.3) As always, pressing `[Esc]` takes you back 'up', out of the report itself to the form. What about the options available along the bottom of the form? Let's have a look at the first of them, Layout, selected with `[F7]`.

```
                         Create Summary Report

  Report title (optional): Cash Flow Report

  Restrict to transactions from:  1/ 1/93 through: 31/ 3/93

  Row headings (down the left side): 1
        1. Category           3. Description
        2. Class              4. Account

  Column headings (across the top): 1
        1. Don't Subtotal     5. Month             9. Category
        2. Week               6. Quarter          10. Class
        3. Two Weeks          7. Six Months       11. Description
        4. Half Month         8. Year             12. Account

  Use Current/All/Selected accounts (C/A/S): S

 Esc-Cancel               F8-Options  F9-Filter              ◄┘ Continue
```

Fig. 4.7. Report Layout Screen

You will find a fuller version of the form you have just left. This time, you can specify the starting and ending day (not just month) for the report. The Cash Flow report we have already looked at summarised all the data for the period in question. The most meaningful change of layout we can make to a Cash Flow report is to ask *Quicken* to organise it month-by-month instead. So choose a date span that includes several months. Pick any starting and ending days you fancy.

The next choice is Row Headings. *Quicken* has filled in a '1', meaning that the row headings down the left side of the report are to be the names of categories, as they were on the Cash Flow report we have just been looking at. There are three other possibilities, as you see: the Row Headings could be Class, Description, or Account. See Chapter Seven, on Shares Investment accounts, and Chapter Nine, on the business uses of *Quicken*, for some suggestions on organising a report by Classes. 'Description' and 'Account' both produce meaningless reports in a Cash Flow context (unless you have organised your accounts in a highly sophisticated and unexpected way), but you might like to choose them anyway and see what happens.

Next comes Column Headings. *Quicken* provides a '1' here as well, meaning 'Don't Subtotal'. We are going to change that for one of the periods of time on offer. Choose '5' for Month, if you have enough data. Later, you might find it interesting to come back and let *Quicken* show you your Cash Flow situation by Quarter and even, eventually, by Year.

Finally, you can decide whether to include all your accounts in this report or only some of them. 'Current' in this context means the account you were working with before you started work on reports. If you choose 'S' for 'Selected', when you finish answering the questions on this screen you will see another screen with a list of your accounts.

Before you leave this window to go on to make your selection of accounts, however, press `[F8]` for the Report Options window. Since this is a Cash Flow Report, you will want it organised on a cash flow basis. You will probably want to choose External Transfers Only from the next offering. Chapter Six, Asset and Liability Accounts, explains what is involved here and includes (Fig 6.4) a view of the Report Options window.

But you might want to play around now with the final choice in this window, 'Normal/Suppressed/Reversed subcategory display.' If you choose Normal, all subcategories will appear in your report. If you choose Suppressed, only the categories, not the subcategories, will appear. And if you choose Reversed, you will get a report in which the subcategory is listed first, before its parent category. This provision, odd at first glance, lets you group together similar subcategories from different parts of your budget. If you have subcategories for Insurance, for example, under both House and Car (ie, House:Insurance and Car:Insurance), this choice would let you group all your Insurance transactions together.

When you have finished with Report Options, you will be back at the Create Summary Report window. When you have answered all the questions there, you be offered the list of your accounts to choose from. There will be a column on the right with the word 'Include' repeated next to each account (meaning, of course, to include that account in the current report).

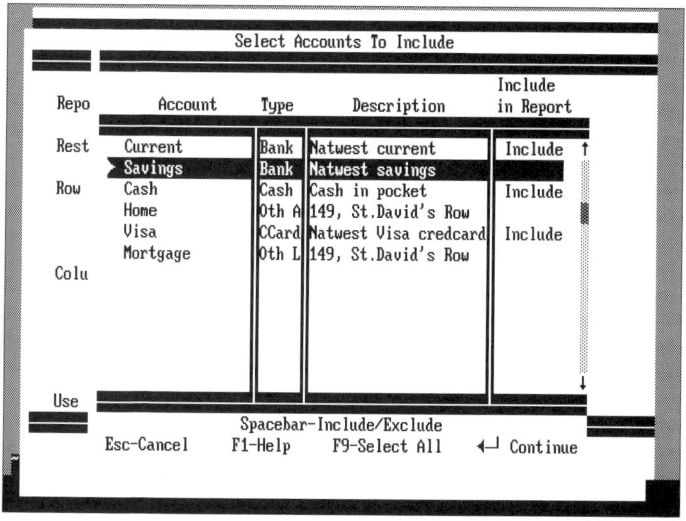

Select Accounts To Include

	Account	Type	Description	Include in Report
Repo				
Rest	Current	Bank	Natwest current	Include
	Savings	Bank	Natwest savings	
Row	Cash	Cash	Cash in pocket	Include
	Home	Oth A	149, St.David's Row	
	Visa	CCard	Natwest Visa credcard	Include
	Mortgage	Oth L	149, St.David's Row	
Colu				
Use				

Spacebar-Include/Exclude

Esc-Cancel F1-Help F9-Select All ↵ Continue

Fig. 4.8. Selecting Accounts

You now move the highlight up and down the list with the arrow keys, and press the space bar when you get to an account you don't want in this report. The word 'Include' vanishes. Pressing the space bar again brings it back. *Quicken* will remember your choices, and not just for this particular report. When you next come back to this screen, it will be as you left it. But if you have quantities of accounts and filter this report down to one or two of them, you won't have to toil through the whole list pressing the space bar to get the others back at some point in the future. Pressing `[F9]` at this screen means 'Include All'.

Now press `[Enter]` until you see your report. This time, your Cash Flow position is reported month by month, as indicated by the column headings at the top of the screen, as well as category by category, still listed down the left hand side. Positioning the highlight over a category and pressing the minus sign condenses the data, just as it did before.

Even with a 43-line display, some of this report will be invisible, off to the right of your computer screen. With a 25-line display, you will only be able to see two months at a time. To move around in your report, remember the Fast Keys mentioned earlier. At the far right of the report when you finally get there you will find a column called OVERALL TOTAL in which the information is summarised. If you now use the minus sign to reduce the whole report to TOTAL INFLOWS and TOTAL OUTFLOWS month by month, you will have a rather interesting view of your financial picture.

```
File/Print   Edit   Layout   Reports   Activities                F1-Help

                         Cash Flow Report

                     1/10/92 Through 31/ 3/93
TEST-Selected Accounts
16/ 3/93

      Category Description                  12/92            1/93
                                       -------------    -------------
TOTAL INFLOWS                               2,429.20         1,876.45
TOTAL OUTFLOWS                              6,434.64         2,723.59
                                          ----------       ----------
OVERALL TOTAL                              -4,005.44          -847.14
                                          ==========       ==========
```

Fig. 4.9. The Bottom Line

Filtering a Report

Press `[Esc]` until you get back to the first screen of choices relating to reports. Choose Personal Reports again, and Cash Flow again from the next menu. This time, on the form where you specify the title and the date range for your report, press `[F9]` to filter it.

You will now see a screen which allows you complete freedom to exclude anything you like from the total picture of your finances. Perhaps you have some income or some expense which 'doesn't really count' – a lot of us do. Perhaps you want to throw some light on one particular corner of life: the amount of interest you earn from your building society account compared to the amount you spend on beer. Anything is possible – at least, it is if you have a separate category or Class for 'beer'.

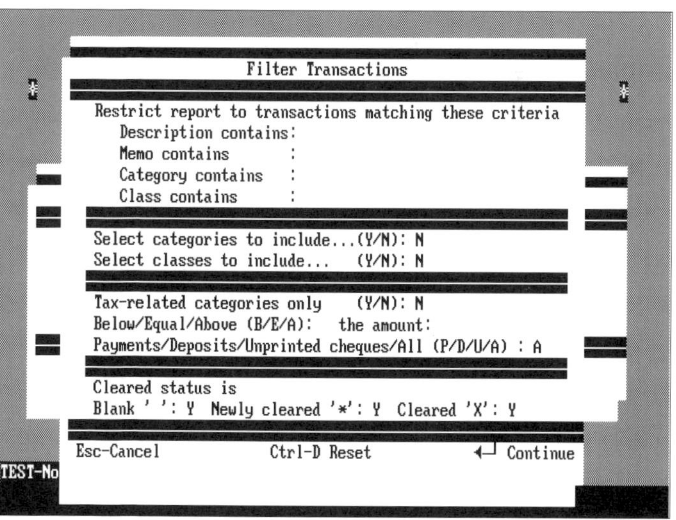
Filter Transactions

Restrict report to transactions matching these criteria
Description contains:
Memo contains :
Category contains :
Class contains :

Select categories to include...(Y/N): N
Select classes to include... (Y/N): N

Tax-related categories only (Y/N): N
Below/Equal/Above (B/E/A): the amount:
Payments/Deposits/Unprinted cheques/All (P/D/U/A) : A

Cleared status is
Blank ' ': Y Newly cleared '*': Y Cleared 'X': Y

Esc-Cancel Ctrl-D Reset ↵ Continue

Fig. 4.10. Filtering a Report

The Filter Transactions screen is easy to understand. First of all, you can tell *Quicken* whether you want the report confined to transactions with a particular description – the 'description' of a transaction is normally the payee, remember – or with a particular memo. Note that the descriptions or memos of your transactions don't have to be absolutely identical to produce useful results here. If you put just one word as the Description or the Memo on this screen, *Quicken* will find all the transactions containing that word.

For example, if you enter your supermarket bill as 'Sainsbury' one week and 'Sainsbury's' or even 'spent at Sainsbury's' the next, you will be able to catch all the entries in your net by putting the word 'Sainsbury' on the filter screen as the Description. Even 'sainsbury' will do the trick – *Quicken* knows that none of us is very consistent in our use of capital letters.

Always try to use the shortest possible word or phrase to do your filtering: *Quicken* will find the entries for 'Sainsbury's' if you filter on 'Sainsbury' but it won't work the other way around: if you put 'Sainsbury's' on the filter screen, you will filter out any transactions which you may have entered as just plain 'Sainsbury' – and that may not be what you intend to do.

If you want your filtered report to contain information on just one category, fill it in when you come to the word 'Category' after 'Description' and 'Memo'. (Anything you don't want to use as a criterion for filtering, just leave blank.) But perhaps you are planning something more ambitious, where certain categories are included but not all. In that case, leave 'Category' blank in the first section of the screen, and answer 'Y' to the question 'Select categories to include' in the next section. You will do the actual selecting when you have finished answering all the questions on this screen.

You can also 'Select classes to include'. 'Classes' in *Quicken* are an advanced feature which you may never need. If you do, they can be very useful indeed.

The rest of the questions are more specifically related to the business of bookkeeping. Do you want to include only tax- related categories? Useful when you are preparing a tax return – see Chapter Eight. Only transactions above, below or equal to a certain amount? Only payments? Only deposits? Only unprinted cheques? That question refers to *Quicken*'s facility for printing your cheques on your computer printer. Is that what is meant by 'a licence to print money'? Alas, no. See Chapter Nine, *Business Use of Quicken*, for more on printing cheques. Finally, you can filter out cheques which have or haven't been cleared through your bank.

Press `[Enter]` repeatedly to speed through the questions you aren't interested in for the present. If you have answered 'Yes' to the question 'Select categories to include', you will next see the screen on which you can do that. All your categories will be listed, both income and expense. Choosing which ones to include or exclude is done in exactly the same way as choosing accounts: move the highlight up and down the list, press the space bar to remove the word 'Include' or to get it back again for any particular category; or press `[F9]` to 'Include all'. And again, *Quicken* will remember your choices for the future.

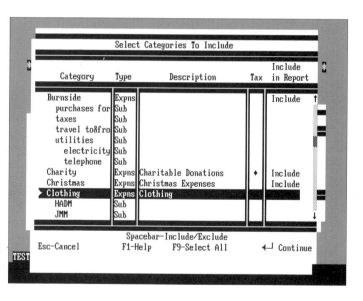

Select Categories To Include

Category	Type	Description	Tax	Include in Report
Burnside	Expns			Include
purchases for	Sub			
taxes	Sub			
travel to&fro	Sub			
utilities	Sub			
electricity	Sub			
telephone	Sub			
Charity	Expns	Charitable Donations	♦	Include
Christmas	Expns	Christmas Expenses		Include
Clothing	Expns	Clothing		
HADM	Sub			
JMM	Sub			

Spacebar-Include/Exclude
Esc-Cancel F1-Help F9-Select All ↵ Continue

TEST

Fig. 4.11 Selecting Categories

Now press `[Enter]` as before, until you see your filtered Cash Flow report.

Memorising a report: Perhaps you will find this display so useful that you decide you want to be able to come back to it quickly in the future, without having to answer questions and make choices. Simply press **[Ctrl]-[M]** while the report is visible on the screen. If you haven't yet given it a name, *Quicken* will ask you to do so now. If you accidentally choose a name that you have already given to another memorised report, *Quicken* will remind you. That's all. The program will give three quick beeps, meaning heard-and-understood. Your report is memorised. From now on, you will find it listed under the name you gave it when you choose Memorised Reports from the first screen of choices connected with reports.

There are two things to note here: The Ctrl-M option for memorising a report is not actually mentioned on the *Quicken* screen when you need it. This is one of the rare instances in *Quicken* when you need to remember what to do – or look it up. Pressing **[F1]** for Help will produce the information. Secondly, although the program has memorised the format for you, it does not memorise the actual data. When you choose your memorised format by name in the future, you will be asked for the date range you want covered. And one further point before we continue with a quick tour of the other report formats. Up to now, we have been making decisions about the format of our Cash Flow reports and then generating the reports. But you can do it the other way around – generate the report first, and then change the layout or format in any way you like. If you use **[Alt]-[E]**, **[Alt]-[L]** or **[Alt]-[A]** to choose 'Edit', 'Layout' or 'Activities' from the toolbar, you can then choose any or all of the operations we have been looking at in the last few pages. And when you have told *Quicken* your requirements, the program will pause for a moment, and then generate a new report to your new specifications.

Other Report Formats

What about the other possible Personal Reports, besides Cash Flow? If you have a report or a Transaction Register on- screen, press **[Alt]-[R]** to access the Reports menu and then choose Personal Reports. Or press **[Esc]** to get back to the Main Menu and then go 'down' again through Create Reports to Personal Reports and then to the Personal Reports menu.

Here are the other possibilities.

Monthly Budget: This report lists budgeted and actual amounts side by side, month by month, with a third column showing the difference between the two. Although it is called 'Monthly Budget', you can use the choices accessed under 'Layout' to set any other period you prefer. `[Alt]-[L]` to get the Layout Menu from the toolbar while you have a Monthly Budget report on screen; or `[F7]` for Layout from the preliminary screen.) You will find as you start working seriously with *Quicken*, if you didn't know already, that life is one damned thing after another. Putting it in financial terms, at least one large unexpected expense turns up most months. A quarterly comparison of budgets with actuals may give a fairer picture than a monthly one.

Again, you can position the highlight over the category names on the right-hand side of the screen and press the minus sign to force *Quicken* to summarise your accounts under fewer headings. Then if (when) you find that you were miles over the budget last month, you can reinstate the category names with the plus sign and go through them carefully to find the trouble spots. Remember that when you put the highlight over a figure, you can press `[Ctrl]-[Z]` to get a list of actual transactions. How could we have spent so much on entertainment last month? Oh, yes.

If you set the end-date for a Monthly Budget report to some time in the future, you can use it to look ahead and predict the horrible months when all your bills turn up at once. But the Monthly Budget report is not ideally suited for peering into the future. The 'Actual' and 'Difference' columns fill up too much of the screen and make it difficult to pick out the information you want. Better to go straight to the Budget screen and look at the Total Budget Inflows/ Total Budget Outflows lines which are always visible at the bottom of that screen. (To see the Budget screen: `[Alt]-[A]` for the Activities menu from any Transaction Register; then Set Up Budgets from that menu.)

temised Categories: If you choose this one without any filters you will get an enormous report listing every transaction under every category for the period of time you specify. Filtered down to one or two categories, Descriptions or Memos, however, it makes an excellent way to direct a spotlight onto a murky corner of your financial life. You will probably want to have *Quicken* memorise several filtered Itemised Category reports for your future use. (**[Alt]-[M]** while the report is on-screen.)

Tax Summary: We'll leave this one for Chapter Eight, where tax matters are discussed.

Net Worth: This one is short and simple. *Quicken* looks at the state of all your accounts, adds up the plusses and subtracts the minuses, and tells you the answer. If you have included asset and liability accounts (see Chapter Six) this report will give you an overall picture of your financial standing, as accurate as the information you have provided. If you have put only your bank accounts and building societies and credit cards into the program, this report will show you how much cash you have to your name.

If you have to go talk to a bank manager about a loan, take along a *Quicken* Net Worth report. It will make an impression. This report can also be useful when you are planning a savings and investment strategy.

Missing Cheque: This report lists all the transactions for the specified period in order of the cheque number. If a number is duplicated or missing in the sequence, the program points it out.

Obviously, your cheques were correctly numbered by the bank, or by the program itself, if you are using *Quicken* to print your cheques. This point of this report is to find mistakes you made in entering transactions. A 'missing cheque' in the other sense, the one you wrote two months ago and are beginning to hope may never be presented, will show up when you are reconciling your bank statement – see Chapter Five.

To print a report, first ensure that the report itself is to your liking on the computer screen, and make sure, too, that the printer is turned on and supplied with paper. Then

NET WORTH REPORT
As of 16/07/93

Acct	Balance
ASSETS	
Cash and Bank Accounts	
Cash	36.55
Current	873.77
Savings	4,500.00
Total Cash and Bank Accounts	5,410.32
Other Assets	
Home	153,374,67
Total Other Assets	153,374,67
TOTAL ASSETS	**158,784.99**
LIABILITIES	
Credt Cards	
Visa	465.67
Total Credit Cards	465.67
Other Liabilities	
Mortgage	122,732.22
Total Other Liabilities	122,732.22
TOTAL LIABILITIES	**123,227.89**
TOTAL NET WORTH	**35,557.10**

press [Ctrl]-[P] to see the Print Report menu. You have to choose a printer or alternatively tell *Quicken* to 'print' the report to disk in a format your word-processor or spreadsheet can use.

If the report is too wide to fit on your computer screen, it is also too wide to fit on a standard sheet of A4 paper. There are several ways round this problem:

● If your printer is capable of condensed type, you can squeeze more than half as much again on to the page. When you installed your printer for use with *Quicken*, the program 'knew' whether condensed type was possible. If it is, that choice will be listed among the options on the Print Report menu, rather as if your condensed-type printer were a separate machine. Choose that, and *Quicken* will do the rest.

● A laser printer capable of printing landscape-style can squeeze in even more. Again, *Quicken* will know from your printer installation choices whether that is possible, and offer it as an option on the Print Report menu.

● Or you may have a wide-carriage printer. Again, *Quicken* will know.

● If you still want to print a report which is too wide for the printer, *Quicken* will 'know' that, too, and will print the report on the paper available in a way that will let you assemble the sheets side-by-side and tape them together for a wide report.

See Chapter One on the subject of installing printers. Some of the most useful reports, such as Cash Flow and Monthly Budget for one month, fit nicely onto A4 paper.

Tips:

● Make a habit of frequently consulting a month-by-month Cash Flow report reduced to essentials: TOTAL INFLOWS minus TOTAL OUTFLOWS. If the news is bad, have a hard look, category by category, at a Monthly Budget report to see where in particular you are spending more than you anticipated. Go back to the Budget screen regularly to inspect your anticipated cash flow in months ahead. Keeping control of cash flow is, in the end, what money management is all about.

● Have *Quicken* memorise some Itemised Transaction reports filtered down to one particular category, subcategory or sub-subcategory you want to monitor closely. You might want to know how much you are spending on a hobby, for example, or how much the car really costs.

● Once you've got the hang of the *Quicken* report system, finding and organising information is so easy that you may never need to print a report. But many people find that regular printed reports kept in a file or ring binder are a powerful aid to budgeting and account-keeping. Don't rush in to anything – too much paper is worse than none. Take a few months to try out different report formats while building up your data. You can always go back to the beginning and print out a report for each month of your accounts when you know exactly what you want.

● See Chapters Seven and Eight for help with specialised reports for investment and tax purposes.

Graphs

Graphs are colourful, they're fun, and you may spot something about your finances which you hadn't cottoned on to from tables of figures. *Quicken* can draw a lot of different graphs, and *Quicken for Windows* is even better than the MS-DOS version in this respect. It's worth exploring the possibilities thoroughly, and returning to the ones you find helpful. The techniques you learned while working on reports can be used, in simplified form, to filter data for your graphs. You can select the date range; accounts; categories and Classes (but not Descriptions and Memos); and amounts (so that your graph only includes transactions above or below an amount you name).

Quicken for Windows **allows you to see two graphs at once, if you like, and will also print your graphs if your printer is up to it.**

Types of Graph

There are essentially four types of graph in Quicken:

● **pie charts**, in which each item is a different- coloured and different-sized slice of pie;

- **line graphs**, showing (for example) how the value of your BT shares changes with time;

- **double-bar graphs**, comparing two items such as Income and Expenditure or Budget and Actual with each other.

- **stacked bar graphs**, in which the individual bars are made up of different-coloured and different-sized sections similar to a pie chart, and the size of the different bars compared with each other is also significant. These graphs can thus show two trends simultaneously.

Quicken will draw all these graphs in colour if your computer has a colour monitor, or in different patterns if your monitor is black-and-white. Choose Set Preferences from the main menu to make changes, and see Chapter Ten, *Nuts and Bolts*, for details. You can also press **[F8]**, 'Setup', and make more changes from the screen on which you set the date range for your graph.

The complete roll-call of possible variations on these themes is a long one.

TIP: You'll enjoy exploring graphs. Whenever you notice something that surprises you, go to a report and find the actual figures behind the graph. Try to work out the reason for your surprise. In *Quicken for Windows*, you can click on a section of a pie chart or stacked bar graph and see the actual figures at once.

When you choose View Graphs from the main menu, the next set of choices (we'll call it Graphs One) is

Income and Expense
Net Worth

Budget and Actual

Investment

If you choose Income and Expense from Graphs One, the next set of choices is headed Income and Expense Graphs:

Monthly Income and Expense
Monthly Income Less Expense

Income Composition
Income Trend

Expense Composition
Expense Trend

We'll work down the list.

Monthly Income and Expense: This is a simple double-bar graph showing income and expenses, one double-bar for each of the months in the time span you specify. You hope that Income, yellow, is bigger than Expenses, blue.

Monthly Income Less Expense: A line graph, with one point for each of the months in your time span. All is well while the points on the line are above zero.

Income Composition: A pie chart in which each slice represents a different source of income, if you are lucky enough to have different sources of income. You can choose the number of categories for the pie, between 2 and 12; and whether or not to have the remaining ones lumped together as 'Other'.

Income Trend: A stacked bar graph in which the different-coloured sections of the bars represent different sources of income, and the height of the bars represents total income. If you have deposit or building society accounts and data covering 1992 and early 1993, you can see graphically how the successive reduction in interest rates has reduced that part of your income – and reduced the total as well, unless you had some good luck to make up for it.

Expense Composition: A pie chart in which each slice represents a different category of expense. You have the same choices as for the Income Composition pie. This chart is especially useful at showing the distortions which can be caused by one or two enormous bills.

Expense Trend: A stacked bar graph in which the different-coloured sections of the bars represent different categories of expense, and the height of the bars represents total expense. This is one of the most useful of all the graphs. Some items such as 'Food' are usually of fairly constant size from one bar to the next; while others assume enormous importance one month and vanish the next.

Now we must go back up a level, to Graphs One, and choose the next item on that list, Net Worth. Remember, Net Worth reports and graphs will be more significant if you have set up Asset and Liability accounts as described in Chapter Six. But even if you have only told *Quicken* about your bank and building society accounts and your credit and store cards, these graphs will not be entirely without interest. The Net Worth Graphs screen follows the same pattern as Income and Expense Graphs:

Monthly Assets and Liabilities
Monthly Assets less Liabilities

Asset Composition
Asset Trend

Liability Composition
Liability Trend

Monthly Assets and Liabilities: A double-bar graph in which Assets (bank accounts, cash on hand, or things such as the value of your house or your stamp collection) are yellow and good; compared with Liabilities (overdrafts, credit and store card debts, balance owed on your mortgage), which are blue and bad.

Monthly Assets less Liabilities: A line graph, with a point for each month. As long as the line is above zero, your assets must add up to at least a little bit more than your liabilities. The negative equity which many householders experienced in 1992 and 1993, where the amount owed on a mortgage was more than the current market value of the house, would show up on this graph as a grim plunge below zero.

Asset Composition: A pie chart in which each slice represents one of your assets.

Asset Trend: A stacked bar graph in which each section represents a different asset and the height of the bars represents your total wealth as known to *Quicken*. You will see the height of the bars sink when you dip in to your savings to pay for a holiday; or rise when the stockmarket sends the value of your holdings through the roof.

Liability Composition: A pie chart in which each slice represents a different liability.

Liability Trend: A stacked bar chart in which the different coloured sections of the bars represent different liabilities, and the height of the bars represents total indebtedness. If you filter this one down to one credit card, you will get a quick view of how the amount you owe Visa or Access has varied from one month to the next.

Again, go back up a level to Graphs One. This time, choose Budget and Actual. The new menu will be:

Monthly Budget and Actual
Monthly Actual less Budget

Categories Over Budget
Categories Under Budget

Budget Composition
Budget Trend

Monthly Budget and Actual: A double-bar graph comparing budget (yellow) with actual (blue) expenses, or income, or both. This and other budget graphs make better sense if you look at income and expense separately. This one will give you a good idea of how accurate your budgeting is.

Monthly Actual less Budget: A line graph with a point for each month of your data. The higher the line goes, the more your spending went over budget. Any points below zero on this graph are good news indeed – you brought a whole month in under budget.

Categories over Budget: A double-bar graph showing the main categories (income or expense) which went over-budget. The comparison between the budget and the actual bars gives you an idea how far over budget you were.

Categories Under Budget: Same again, this time showing which categories were under budget.

Budget Composition: A pie chart showing, for the whole period of time under consideration, each of your major budget categories as a different-coloured pie slice. *Quicken 6.0* does not print graphs (although *Quicken for Windows* does), so there is no way other than a good visual memory to compare this with the Expense Trend pie chart.

Budget Trend: A stacked bar chart with your budget categories as the sections of the bars. The height of the bars shows the different amount budgeted for each month. Like its 'sister' chart, Expense Trend, this one is particularly interesting.

For the final choice on Graphs One, Investment, see Chapter Seven.

CHAPTER

Advanced topics

FEATURING

- Reconciling a bank or credit card statement
- Completing a financial year
- Memorised transactions
- Billminder
- Foreign currencies

By now you know all you need to know for the day-to-day and week-by-week use of *Quicken*. This chapter explores activities which occur less frequently: reconciling your bank and credit card statements; and closing out the financial year. There is something here, too, about optional aspects of the program: memorising transactions you make frequently, working with foreign currencies, and letting *Quicken* remind you when to pay your bills. Further features, including *Quicken*'s willingness to print your cheques and to memorise groups of transactions which occur at the same time, are discussed in Chapter Nine, *Business Uses of Quicken*. These features are available and indeed were intended for domestic users. Be sure to look at that chapter to see if there is anything there for you.

Reconciling a Bank (or Credit Card) Statement

When a bank statement arrives, you may be in the habit of taking one quick, horrified look to see how low was the lowest ebb before stuffing it out of sight. Now that you have taken control of your financial life with *Quicken*, it is time to face up to bank statements as well. Don't believe it? Try talking to a few people who use a budget program, not necessarily *Quicken*. You will hear stories of mistakes on bank statements and credit card accounts, 'and I never would have caught it if I hadn't been using...' Assume we are reconciling a current account. Gather up all your Switch vouchers and, if you are fortunate enough to have a bank which issues them, the advice slips for withdrawals you made from cash machines. You will want your cheque book as well, for the information on the stubs.

Then, bank statement in hand, choose the Transaction Register for the account you want to reconcile, and choose Reconcile from the Activities menu in the toolbar. You will start with a screen in which to check and to enter some important preliminary information

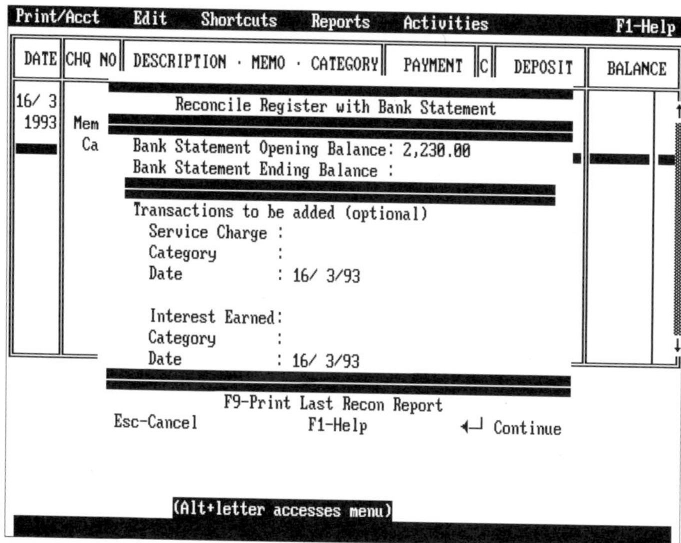

Fig. 5.1. First Reconciliation Screen

Quicken shows you on this form, first of all, the 'Bank Statement Opening Balance'. If this is your first reconciliation, that was the amount you told *Quicken* was in the account when you first set it up. It ought to be right, as you copied it from the end of your previous bank statement. If there should be a mistake, you can correct it now. In the future, *Quicken* takes the 'Opening Balance' of each reconciliation from the 'Closing Balance' of the last one.

Next, you must supply the Closing Balance from the statement you are about to reconcile.

Then *Quicken* invites you to look at the statement and find an entry for a service charge the bank may have decided to help itself to; or (happy thought) an interest payment you have been credited with. Both can be filled in on this screen, and assigned to categories. *Quicken* will have filled in the current day's date, but you can change that to the date listed on the statement for the charge or credit.

When that is done, press `[Enter]` for the Reconciliation window.

At the top are listed the uncleared transactions in the account you are dealing with. If this is your first reconciliation, all the transactions except the opening balance will be uncleared. At the bottom of the screen is the Reconciliation Summary: keep an eye on it as you proceed; you will find it extremely helpful.

Print/Acct Edit Shortcuts Reports Activities F1-Help

CHQ NO	C	AMOUNT	DATE	DESCRIPTION	MEMO
		2,425.00	4/ 9/92	Pay deposit	
		-2,000.00	5/ 9/92	Transfer	
		-100.00	9/ 9/92	Cash dispenser withdra	
202001		-59.97	2/ 9/92	Weirmouth Electricity	
202002		-185.98	2/ 9/92	Central Market	
202003		-1,158.39	9/ 9/92	British Home Mortgage	
202004		-241.89	21/ 9/92	Natwest Visa	
202005		-35.00	21/ 9/92	British Telecommunicat	

←┘-Mark Cleared Item ▪ SpaceBar-UnMark Item ▪ F9-Add or Change Items

RECONCILIATION SUMMARY

Items You Have Marked Cleared (*)

			Cleared (X,*) Balance	2,230.00
0	Cheques, Debits	0.00	Bank Statement Balance	753.46
0	Deposits, Credits	0.00	Difference	1,476.54

F1-Help F8-Mark Range F9-View Register Ctrl-F Find Ctrl F10-Done

Fig. 5.2. Reconciling a Bank Statement

The most important figures in the summary are in the bottom right-hand corner: the **Cleared Balance,** which starts as the opening balance you have just agreed on the preceding screen, and changes every time you mark your item as cleared; and the **Bank Statement Balance**, which is the amount you copied from the new statement onto the preceding screen; and the difference. When the difference is 0, your job is done.

On the left, the summary shows you separately the totals of the debits and the credits you have so far marked as cleared. Accountants may be dismayed but the rest of us will not be at all sorry to discover that the words 'Debit' and 'Credit' to *Quicken* mean what they mean in the real world: debits make the balance in your account less (or your overdraft greater); credits do the opposite.

Your task is to move the highlight to each of the listed transactions in turn and press `[Enter]` to mark it as cleared if you find it on your bank statement. If you mark one by mistake, position the highlight on it again and press the spacebar to unmark it.

This will work best if you look for the transactions in the order they appear on the bank statement, NOT the order in which they appear on the *Quicken* reconciliation screen. You probably entered the transactions in *Quicken* more or less as they were made; but cheques can sometimes take a surprising length of time to appear on your statement. You will notice that *Quicken* lists your cheques on this reconciliation screen separately from your Switch payments and cash withdrawals anyway, so you will have to skip around a bit to find each item.

Put the statement flat on the desk beside your computer, put a ruler under the first transaction to make sure that your bleary eyes read the line straight across, and start to work. As you find each transaction in *Quicken* and mark it cleared, tick it off on the bank statement and move the ruler down.

As you come to entries on the bank statement for Switch payments and cash withdrawals, check them against your advice slips as well as locating them in *Quicken*.

Withdrawals from cash machines are especially tricky. Like most people, you probably withdraw the same amount fairly frequently but at irregular intervals. If you have advice slips, compare them closely with the statement to check both the amount and the date and time at which the withdrawal was made. If, during your first reconciliation session, you find it difficult to match up the withdrawals on the statement with the withdrawals you have entered in *Quicken*, resolve in future to enter more detail (such as the time and place of the withdrawal) in *Quicken*. Horror stories in the newspapers of 'phantom withdrawals' may overstate the danger. Who knows? But now that you are using *Quicken*, you might as well be very careful about cash withdrawals.

Incidentally, the need to keep a check on cash machines is

an argument in favour of maintaining a cash account in *Quicken*. If you have a cash account, you can't 'forget' a withdrawal without throwing the cash account out of balance by the same amount. See Chapter Two for a discussion of cash accounts and the various ways this problem can be handled.

Unless you are a financial wizard of the first water, you are likely to need to make some changes in your records before you will be able to balance the statement. Probably there will be one or two transactions you simply left out. There are likely to be ghostly cheques which you wrote before you started using *Quicken*, now returning to haunt you. This is especially true when you are reconciling a bank statement for the first time. There could be Standing Order or Direct Debit payments which you had forgotten were due last month. There could be amounts you have typed in wrongly – but do double-check on this one; maybe your records are right and the bank is wrong.

You can't make changes from the Reconciliation screen. Press `[F9]` to go to the Transaction Register of the account you are working with. There, you can make any additions or alterations necessary. If the problem is due to a Standing Order or Direct Debit which you had forgotten about, you can and should choose Standing Orders from the Shortcuts menu on the toolbar right now and enter it, so that *Quicken* can look after it in the future.

While you are working in the Transaction Register, the Reconciliation Summary remains visible at the bottom of the screen, just to remind you what is going on. When you are ready to go on reconciling the bank statement, press `[F9]` again.

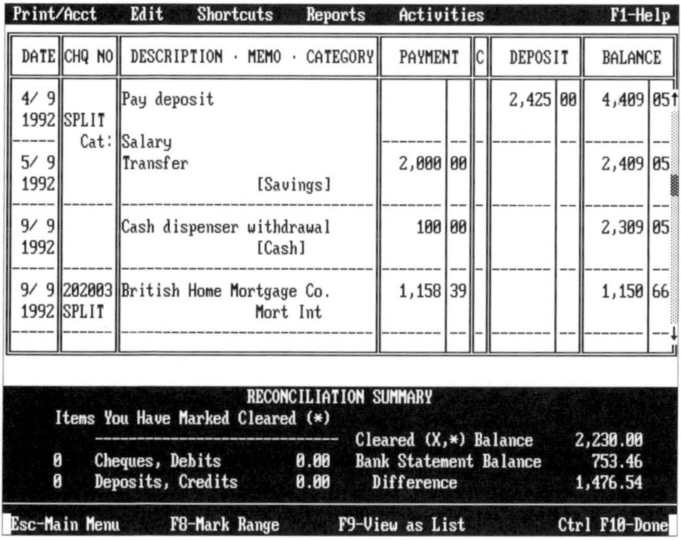

```
Print/Acct  Edit  Shortcuts  Reports  Activities                    F1-Help

DATE | CHQ NO | DESCRIPTION · MEMO · CATEGORY | PAYMENT   | C | DEPOSIT  | BALANCE
4/ 9 |        | Pay deposit                   |           |   | 2,425 00 | 4,409 05
1992 | SPLIT  |                               |           |   |          |
-----|   Cat: | Salary                        |           |   |          |
5/ 9 |        | Transfer                      | 2,000 00  |   |          | 2,409 05
1992 |        |                     [Savings] |           |   |          |
9/ 9 |        | Cash dispenser withdrawal     |   100 00  |   |          | 2,309 05
1992 |        |                        [Cash] |           |   |          |
9/ 9 | 202003 | British Home Mortgage Co.     | 1,158 39  |   |          | 1,150 66
1992 | SPLIT  |                      Mort Int |           |   |          |

                        RECONCILIATION SUMMARY
   Items You Have Marked Cleared (*)
                                    Cleared (X,*) Balance       2,230.00
   0   Cheques, Debits      0.00    Bank Statement Balance        753.46
   0   Deposits, Credits    0.00      Difference                1,476.54

Esc-Main Menu     F8-Mark Range     F9-View as List          Ctrl F10-Done
```

Fig. 5.3. Transaction Register During Reconciliation

This is one of the very few places where *Quicken* is slightly less than crystal clear in its on-screen help. Your instinct might well be to go back to the reconciliation screen by pressing `[Esc]`. But if you do press `[Esc]` this time, instead of getting where you want to go, you are likely to get into a muddle. *Quicken* will think you want to stop the reconciliation process, and it will not be immediately obvious what to do to tell it otherwise. (Answer: press `[Esc]` again.)

If you have made any changes to transactions you have already marked as cleared, they remain cleared, although the totals at the bottom of the screen will have changed.

When you have worked your way through the bank statement, look again at the figures in the lower right hand corner of the screen. If 'Difference' is now zero, all is well. Press `[Ctrl]-[F10]` and the job is done. *Quicken* will offer to print a reconciliation report, summarising or listing, as you prefer, all the cleared transactions and listing the ones that haven't cleared yet. That can be a valuable reminder of cheques still hanging over your head from past months, as well as providing a list of cheques written too recently to have cleared. It is probably a good idea to let *Quicken* print this report for you the first few times you succeed in reconciling a statement. Use it when you next do a reconciliation. You will soon get to be so good at this sort of thing that you no longer need such help.

But what if 'Difference' at the bottom of the screen is not zero? If the sum involved is trivial – and only you can decide what 'trivial' means in this context – press `[Ctrl]-[F10]` anyway. The program will urge you politely but quite firmly to go back and find the mistake. If you insist, though, it will create a Balance Adjustment Entry, allow you to assign it to a category, and add it to the account. If you find the mistake later, you can always correct it and remove the Balance Adjustment Entry.

If you decide to take the nobler course and try to find the mistake, start off with the figures in the lower left-hand corner of the Reconciliation screen. There, *Quicken* shows you how many debits and how many credits you have marked as cleared, and what is the total of each. Start with credits: there are probably fewer of them. Count the number on the bank statement. Does it agree with *Quicken*'s number? The bank statement probably shows the total amount of credits. Does that agree with *Quicken*'s total? Now do the same for debits – is the number right? Is the total right? By now you should have some idea where the mistake is. If the number of credits or of debits doesn't match, you've left something out or marked as cleared something you shouldn't have. If the total of one or other or both amounts is wrong, there are various possibilities:

- You or the bank has entered the figures wrongly. Look for transposed digits such as '£56.23' for '£65.23'. Look for the digits '0' and'8' which can easily be confused on a computer screen. And when you do find such a mistake, don't be too quick to assume the mistake is yours. It could be the bank's. Look again at chequebook stubs or Switch advice slips.

- You have marked something as cleared which closely resembles an uncleared cheque to the same payee. This is a common pitfall if you have a number of similar cheques to a supermarket or a garage, for instance.

● Perhaps you marked a regular payment without examining it. Was there an unexpected deduction from your pay this month? Was one of your Direct Debits altered by the payee? – Don't forget the ultimate possibility, that all your work is right but you typed the Closing Balance from your bank statement in wrongly. In that case, you will have to press `[Esc]` to stop the reconciliation process and start again. *Quicken* will remember everything you have marked as cleared.

You can sure that *Quicken*'s arithmetic is right; and pretty sure that the bank's arithmetic is too. Beyond that, the only comfort as you struggle is the knowledge that it really does get easier. By the time you have done two or three monthly statements, you will be able to cruise through reconciliation in 10 minutes or so.

Reconciling a Credit Card Statement

This is exactly the same. If you enter all your credit card and store card transactions in *Quicken* as life goes along, reconciling the monthly statements when they come is done in exactly the same way as reconciling a bank statement. The program understands that the balance on a credit card is negative. But perhaps you don't want to be fanatically conscientious over your credit card. You could, for instance:

● Only enter the transactions when the statement arrives, copying them from the statement into *Quicken* and assigning them to categories as you go along. In that case, you can type the asterisk, `[*]`, meaning 'Cleared', into the column headed 'C' while you're about it.

● Go through the reconciliation process marking the transactions you have entered during the month, and then have *Quicken* make a balance adjustment to cover the rest.

● Press `[F8]` from the reconciliation screen. You will then be able to enter a range of dates and *Quicken* will mark as cleared all credit card transactions between those dates.

There's much to be said for treating credit cards and store cards as seriously as a current account, entering every item and checking when the statement comes. But *Quicken* doesn't set itself up to be your mother. If you want to keep dirty socks under the bed, and take BarclayCard's word for how much you owe them, that's up to you.

Completing a Financial Year

Relax: with *Quicken* you don't have to. You can just go on and on adding transactions forever. The authors of the program say that there is room for about 30,000 transactions in any one account, and for more than 65,000 in any one file, taking all the accounts in the file together. They reckon that an average home user will record up to 1,000 transactions a year, and a small business user perhaps up to 3,000. So you can clearly keep going for quite a while before you bump up against the limit.

And it is useful to have a lot of data handy. You can construct reports in which you compare a whole year's finances with another year. You can try out various possibilities, constructing reports by financial quarter or by the half-year and discovering for yourself which gives the most informative picture. You can do a quick search backwards to find the bills connected with a major expense such as a home extension, even though it was finished two or three years ago. When you're working on your tax return, you can have all the data for the last tax year and the one before immediately available.

On the other hand, there may come a time when you feel you would like to pack some old records away with the electronic equivalent of a red ribbon tied around them. Although *Quicken* uses computer memory and disk storage space efficiently, you may eventually reach the point where it takes two or more floppy disks to make regular backups of your data; or where you feel the program has got so much to remember that it is becoming heavy and slow. *Quicken* is ready to be helpful, as ever.

From the main menu, choose set Preferences; from the Preferences menu, choose File Activities; and from File Activities, choose Year End. You can now choose '1' for Archive or '2' for Start New Year.

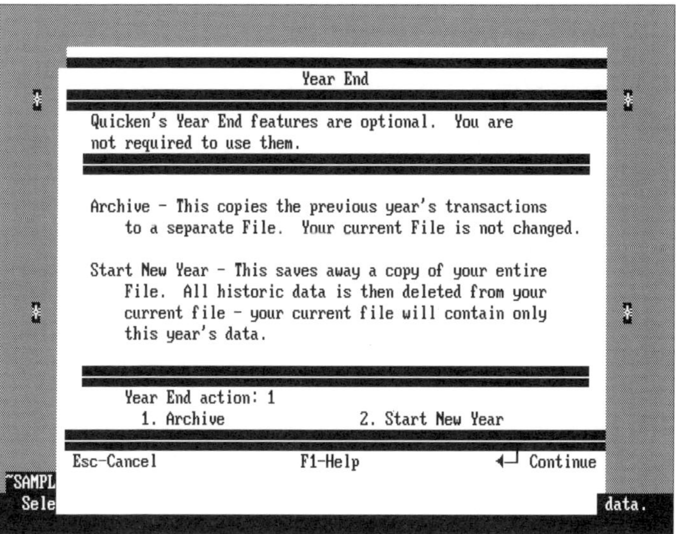
Year End

Quicken's Year End features are optional. You are not required to use them.

Archive - This copies the previous year's transactions to a separate File. Your current File is not changed.

Start New Year - This saves away a copy of your entire File. All historic data is then deleted from your current file - your current file will contain only this year's data.

Year End action: 1
1. Archive 2. Start New Year

Esc-Cancel F1-Help ↵ Continue

Fig. 5.4. Year End Screen

Quicken assumes, whichever choice you make, that you will want your archives to contain the data for complete calendar years. A British taxpayer, however, would be foolish indeed to split such carefully-saved data into calender years – what matters here is income tax years, which run from April 6 of one year until April 5 of the next.

Fortunately, *Quicken* always lets you override its assumptions.

If you choose '1' from the Year End menu, you will next see the Archive File screen. You will have to replace the suggested '31.12.92' (or whatever the last calendar year was) with '5.4.93' so that the archive contains complete tax years. This option does not make your working file any smaller: it simply creates an archive file for added security.

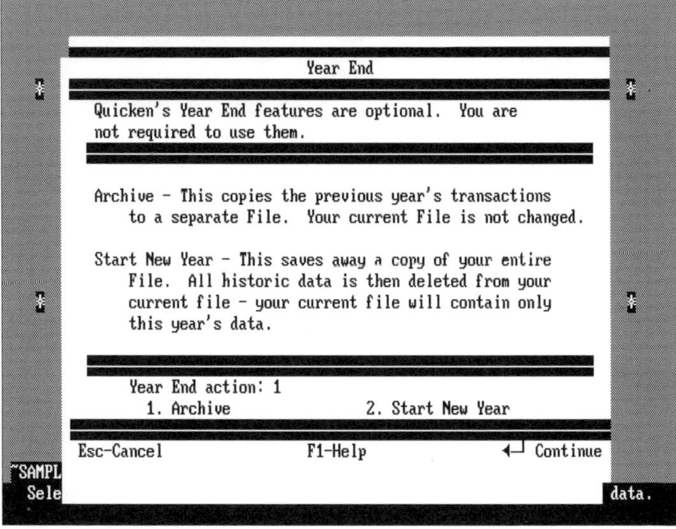

Fig. 5.5. Archive File Screen

But if you choose '2', Start New Year', *Quicken* will make a complete copy of your current file; and will then delete from your current file all transactions not of the current year. Again, you will have to correct the program's quaint American notion that last year ended on December 31; and again, that is easy to do simply by typing in the date of the end of the previous tax year instead. You will have to give a name to your archive file – call it something like 'Tax92-3'. The program will not delete from the current file any uncleared transactions or any investment transactions.

You can make your archive file 'read-only', if you like, so that it cannot be changed. See Chapter 10, *Nuts and Bolts*, for the process. If you have gone through this procedure immediately after the end of the tax year, it might be better to wait a few weeks before making the archive file read-only in case some extra transactions come wandering home like little lost lambs.

Memorising

Anything you do repetitively, *Quicken* can do for you by memorising your input.

You can tell *Quicken* to memorise transactions, report formats, cheques (if you use the program to print your cheques), and groups of transactions.

To memorise a **transaction,** fill in the details in the Transaction Register in the usual way. Press `[Ctrl]-[M]`. *Quicken* will highlight the information which is about to be memorised and ask for confirmation. Then when you next come to pay the gas board or Tesco's or whoever it was, press `[Ctrl]-[T]` to see the list of transactions. Move the highlight to the one you want and press `[Enter]`. *Quicken* copies the entry into the register and waits for you to confirm it with `[Ctrl]-[Enter]` in the usual way. You can either memorise the transaction without an amount, and fill that in each time; or memorise a typical transaction and change the actual amount on the day.

To memorise a **report format,** press `[Ctrl]-[M]` while the report is on-screen. See Chapter Four for further details.

To memorise a **cheque,** press `[Ctrl]-[M` while the cheque you have written is on-screen. See Chapter Nine for more about using *Quicken* to write your cheques.
You may want to memorise a **group of transactions** if, for instance, you pay a bit on account to each of your 15 credit cards at the same time each month.

● First of all, memorise the individual transactions in the group. Or the individual cheques: this process works for either transactions or cheques.

● Then, from the Shortcuts menu on the toolbar, choose Transaction Groups. You will see the list of your groups, if you have any, numbered from 1 to 12. Next to each of the unused numbers will be the word '<unused>'. Select the first <unused> number.

● You will see the Describe Group window. Give your group a name, and, if you like, specify how often it will come into operation and when you want to be reminded of the next scheduled payment.

● Then you will see the list of your memorised transactions. Move the highlight to each one you want to include in your group and press the spacebar.

Whenever you want to use one of your groups, press `[Ctrl]-[J]` to see the list and choose the group you want. You can add transactions to a group, or remove some, at any time.

The Billminder

It is possible, using *Quicken*, to print out your cheques on your computer printer. Many American domestic users of the program take advantage of this feature. In this book, the writing of cheques is discussed in Chapter Nine, *Business Uses of Quicken*, on the theory that British households write fewer cheques at home than American ones and are less likely to want to invest in the stationery necessary for computer printing of cheques. (In America, gas, telephone, and electricity bills are paid monthly; many people run half-a-dozen credit cards; and a remarkable amount of shopping is done by mail order from catalogues.) But the program is yours to use as you wish – see the details in Chapter Nine if the idea interests you.

Even if you decide to struggle on with pen, ink and chequebook, however, you might consider a *Quicken* feature called the Billminder. It can be set to remind you of bills when they are due, to help you postpone payment until the strategic last moment.

This is the procedure: from the Main Menu, choose Write Cheques. The next screen is a form that actually looks like a cheque. Fill it out, dating it on the day, however far in the future, when you mean to write the real cheque and send it off. You can 'write' as many cheques as you like in this way, for different dates.

Three days before the date you put on the cheque, a *Quicken* reminder will appear on your computer screen when you switch the machine on, even before you start using *Quicken*. And there will be another reminder on the Main Menu screen when you do start *Quicken*.

Perhaps you don't use your computer regularly and three days is not long enough. The interval is easily adjusted: from the Main Menu, choose Set Preferences. From the Set Preferences menu, choose Automatic Reminder Settings. You can then set any interval between 0 and 30 days.

Once you have actually written the cheque and sent it on its way, you will need to tell *Quicken* to stop reminding you. Otherwise it will go on forever, telling you that you have overdue cheques to print. If you are using *Quicken* to print the actual cheques, that is not a problem: *Quicken* will know that the cheque has been printed and that no more reminding is necessary.

To stop the reminders without printing the cheque, you must delete it. From the Main Menu, choose Write Cheques. You will see a blank cheque, as before. Press the `[PgUp]` (Page Up) key to see the latest cheque in the system: whatever order you 'write' them in, *Quicken* stores cheques in chronological order.

`[Ctrl]-[Home]` takes you to the earliest cheque,
`[PgDn]` (Page Down) to the next cheque,
`[Ctrl]-[End]` to the last cheque, the blank one.

Use these keys to move about until you find the one you want to delete. In the normal course of events, `[Ctrl]-[Home]` should do it, as you will presumably write and dispatch the oldest cheque first.

When you see on the screen the cheque you want to delete, press `[Ctrl]-[D]`. *Quicken* will ask you to confirm that you want to delete it.

If you use the Billminder in this way, you will need to enter the actual cheque in the Transaction Register yourself when you have written it. If *Quicken* is printing the cheques, the entry in the Register is made automatically.

Quicken has a gentler way of reminding you about bills

due. You can enter a postdated payment directly in the Transaction Register. You will see it in the Register below a double line, with the date in fainter type than the dates of the transactions which have already been made. The Current Balance in the lower right-hand corner of the Transaction Register screen will show you how much money you have in your account; the Ending Balance, just below, shows how much you will have when the postdated payments have been made.

If you use the program most days, that may be reminder enough. But when the due day is past, the payment you postdated will automatically join the others in the Transaction Register and may fool you into thinking you paid it. If you're the sort who needs to put the alarm clock out of reach in order to be sure to get up in time, you might be better with the Billminder: it will go on nagging until you turn it off.

Foreign Currencies

One of *Quicken*'s neater tricks is its ability to think in foreign currencies. You may want to enter occasional credit card purchases made abroad on business or holiday trips and have *Quicken* tell you how much you spent in real money. Or you may maintain bank accounts in other currencies, at home or abroad, and want to include them in your general financial picture. *Quicken* can handle that, even allowing you to transfer funds painlessly between accounts in different currencies. And if you are using the program in a country other than Britain, you can define any currency you like as the 'home currency' in which all transactions are made, and into which other currencies are translated.

In order to do any of this, you must first add the currencies you are interested in to *Quicken*'s list if they aren't already there (although they probably are); and you must keep the program up to date with the latest exchange rates.

To see the currency list, press `[Ctrl]-[K]` from the Transaction Register of any account. Use the arrow keys to move through it. You can delete a currency you have no interest in by highlighting it and pressing `[Ctrl]-[D]`.

Quicken will ask you to confirm that you want to delete the currency.

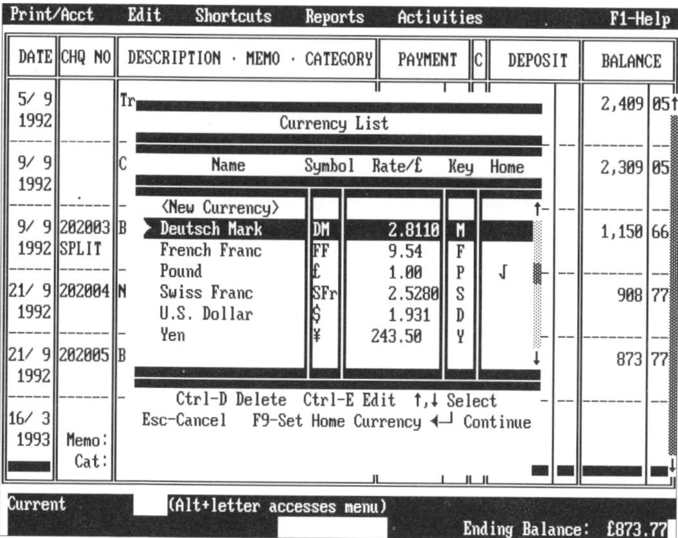

Fig. 5.6. Foreign Currency List

You will see a tick next to the name of your current home currency. If you bought your copy of *Quicken* in Britain, that will be sterling. To choose any other currency instead, highlight it and press `[F9]`.

To add a new currency to the list, move the highlight to <New Currency> at the top of the list and press `[Enter]`. You will need to supply the following information in the Set Up New Currency window:

- The **Currency Name**.

- The **Currency Symbol**. You are allowed up to three characters.

Pounds, dollars and the Japanese Yen have already been provided with the appropriate symbols by *Quicken*. Perfectionists adding a new currency to the list may want to use a symbol which is within the computer's powers but not shown on a standard keyboard. Here's how: one of the manuals supplied with your computer (not the *Quicken* manual) should have a list of ASCII (American Standard Code for Information Interchange) character codes. If you see there a character you want to use as a currency symbol, note its decimal code number. Be sure to get the decimal code – you don't want the 'hex code' or the 'sort sequence'. Then at *Quicken*'s New Currency screen, hold down the `[Alt]` key and type the number for the decimal code.

● Shortcut Letter (optional). This is a one-letter code which tells *Quicken* to convert the amount you have just entered in a Transaction Register into your home currency. For instance, *Quicken* has already suggested 'M' as the shortcut letter for the German mark. If you type '100M' in any register, *Quicken* will enter £42.19, assuming an exchange rate of 2.37 Deutschmarks to the pound.

● Rate. The exchange rate. Normally, you would type in the number of foreign currency units to the pound. Daily papers list these rates for all the common world currencies, usually in a box on one of the business pages.

The *Quicken* Set Up New Currency window shows two exchange rates. Assuming for the moment that you are adding the German Deutschmark to the list (although in fact it is already there), with the Currency Symbol 'DM', you will see 'DM per £', to the left of the window, and '£ per DM' to the right. '£ per DM' is the 'inverse rate' – showing how many pounds you get for one unit of the foreign currency. Normally, you would fill in the left-hand rate, 'DM per £.' *Quicken* will then work out the inverse rate for you. But there may come a day when you find yourself hunched over your portable computer in a Berlin hotel room. Then you may be glad to type in the inverse rate as listed in a local newspaper, showing how many pence sterling to one Deutschmark, and let *Quicken* do the working out in the other direction.

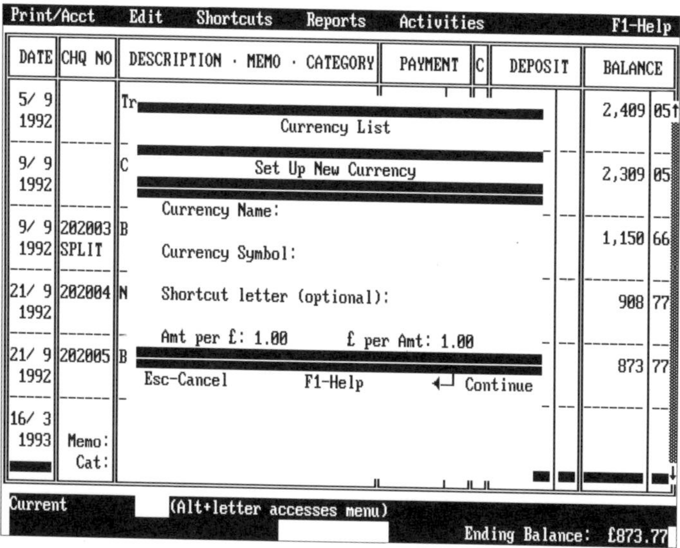

Fig. 5.7. Adding a New Currency

When you have finished filling out the Setting Up New Currency window, press `[Ctrl]-[Enter]` and your new currency will be added to the list. Notice that, to save space, the list does not show the inverse exchange rate, and it gives the rate only to four decimal places. If you have supplied an exchange rate accurate to more decimal places, you can be sure that *Quicken* 'remembers' and will use the more accurate figure in calculations.

You can change any of the details for the currencies on the list in a similar way. Highlight the desired currency and press `[Enter]`. You will see the Edit Currency window, similar to the Setting Up New Currency window. Make any changes you like.

Normally, the one change you will want to make is to the exchange rate. If your foreign currency dealings are rare, you would type in an up-to-date rate only occasionally, just before you enter a foreign currency transaction. If you have business dealings in foreign currencies, you will want to update the rate weekly or even daily.

Once the list is ready it is wonderfully easy to use it.

● To make an **occasional foreign currency entry.** Perhaps you have brought some credit card advice slips back from a trip abroad and want to enter them in *Quicken*; or perhaps you want to send a payment abroad for an item whose price is quoted in a foreign currency.

FIRST: from the Transaction Register of the account you will use for the foreign payment, press `[Ctrl]-[K]` to see the currency list. Move the highlight to the currency in question. Press `[Ctrl]-[E]` for the Edit Currency window. Using today's newspaper for information, correct the exchange rate if necessary. Note the Shortcut Letter for your currency.

THEN: simply enter the transaction in the usual way, putting the shortcut letter immediately after the amount. *Quicken* will translate into pounds. If you have forgotten the shortcut letter, press `[Ctrl]-[K]` for the currency list after typing in the amount; move the highlight to the desired currency; press `[Enter]`.

If you are entering credit card or Eurocheque payments which you have already made, remember to double check the amount when your credit card or bank statement turns up. You can be fairly confident that the bank or the credit card company will have made an extra charge for the currency transaction. The charge may be itemised separately, or it may be concealed in an unfavourable exchange rate. If the charge seems to you peculiarly outrageous, you can try using the evidence of your *Quicken* records to lodge a protest.

To set up a bank account to work entirely in a foreign currency. proceed just as you did when you were setting up your other accounts. (See Chapter Two.) This time, when you get to the Currency field in the Set Up New Account window, press `[Ctrl]-[L]` to see the currency list. Choose a currency from the list. That's it!

You will use your foreign currency account in the ways that are already familiar to you. However, when you make a transfer of funds between accounts in different currencies, *Quicken* has made thoughtful provision for the difficulties of real life.
Enter the transfer in the normal way. Press `[Ctrl]-`

[Enter] as usual to record the transaction. You will see the Foreign Currency Transfer window, with the amount of the transfer in the 'source' currency and the 'destination' currency already filled in, based on the latest exchange rate you have supplied. You may already know that the actual amount which will reach the 'destination' account has been whittled down a bit by bank charges or unfavourable exchange rates, and if so you can make the change now. Otherwise, accept *Quicken*'s figures for the moment. When your bank statements arrive, you can change the transfer amount in either account, source or destination, without affecting the amount in the Transaction Register of the other account.

When you prepare a report in the normal way, *Quicken* will automatically convert your foreign currency account and all its transactions into sterling. But if you would rather have the report in the currency of your foreign account, or, indeed, in any other currency you can think of, choose the Layout Menu by pressing [Alt]-[L] while the report is on the computer screen. If your file contains accounts in different currencies, a 'Report Currency' option is automatically added to the Report Options window. Specify the currency you want.

Transfers between accounts in the same currency normally cancel each other out and should, therefore, be omitted from your summary reports. (See Chapter Four on the whole subject of reports.) But because of fluctuations in exchange rates, movements of funds between accounts in different currencies can involve a gain or a loss. To see how you're doing, include transfers in your report and look for the line 'TOTAL TRANSFERS'. If the transfers were all in one currency, TOTAL TRANSFERS would be zero. If you have been transferring between accounts in different currencies during a period when the exchange rates have been changing, you will see either a positive (you're ahead) or a negative (bad luck) figure next to TOTAL TRANSFERS.

CHAPTER

Asset and liability accounts

FEATURING

- Assets and liabilities defined
- Creating asset accounts
- Valuing assets
- Creating liability accounts

Asset and liability accounts are a special feature of *Quicken*. They have important uses in business accounting: see Chapter Nine. For the rest of us, they are an optional extra. Some of the advice in the section which follows differs from that which you will find in your *Quicken* manual, but on one important point there is complete agreement – it is a good idea to use *Quicken* for some time first, to become familiar with the program and with its benefits in your own particular situation, before striking out into asset and liability accounts. You may decide you don't need them at all.

Assets and Liabilities Defined

A liability account tracks the amount you owe on a debt – the outstanding amount of your mortgage or car loan, for example. You could include more modest hire purchase debts as well.

An asset account records the value of what you own. Current accounts, deposit accounts and building society accounts are all assets. But *Quicken*'s special 'asset accounts' are for assets which are not in the form of ready money. Business users will feel at home here – we're talking about the components of a balance sheet.

There are advantages to recording your assets and liabilities in *Quicken*:

- The Net Worth report becomes considerably more accurate and interesting. You will be able to track the changes (with a bit of luck, the improvement) in your Net Worth through time. You may find it a comfort amidst the buffetings of life.

- If you are thinking of taking on a major loan, a consideration of all the figures may help your decision. Your bank manager will welcome a *Quicken* Net Worth report when consulted about a big loan.

- A careful valuation of your assets, regularly updated, can help you and your financial advisers with some important financial decisions

- about insurance;

- about retirement planning;

- about steps you might take to minimise the effects of Inheritance Tax on your estate;

- about Capital Gains Tax, if you buy and sell assets in a serious way.

Bear in mind as you read the rest of this chapter that a compromise may be possible in your situation. Assets, as you will see, are a good deal easier to handle accurately than liabilities. But if you decide not to have a liability account for your mortgage, you should not list your house in an asset account: obviously, the two are related. The same may well be true of some of your other assets and liabilities: your car and the loan you took out to buy it; anything you are buying on hire purchase; anything you bought with a specific loan which you are still paying off.

One solution would be to have no liability accounts, on the grounds that they are just too complicated; to omit from your accounts all the assets (such as your mortgaged house) which correspond to specific liabilities; but to set up shares investment accounts for your shareholdings (see Chapter Seven) and asset accounts for items like your National Savings Certificates and for valuable possessions which you own outright.

That way, a Net Worth report will give a much more accurate picture of your financial situation than if you had included only current, deposit, cash, and credit card accounts in your records. And you will have the satisfaction of knowing that your actual Net Worth is somewhat higher than *Quicken* thinks, as you also own the fraction of your house and of other assets bought with loans which you have succeeded in paying off to date.

Here are some general guidelines about how to classify your wealth. But always remember:

- that investment offers and opportunities are constantly changing as tax laws change and as financial experts come up with new wheezes; the suggestions that follow do not cover all the possibilities, although they should provide you with some guidelines about classifying investments.

● and that *Quicken* is a highly adaptable program. You don't have to do things the *Quicken* way – you can do them your way. When you have thought about the subject and perhaps experimented a bit, arrange your affairs the way that seems most natural and helpful to you. There's no 'right answer' here.

Assets

Current/Deposit Accounts: use these for any account you put money into and take money out of, such as your current account and your deposit account at the bank; your building society account; your National Savings accounts, both Ordinary and Investment; your Tax Exempt Special Savings Account (TESSA). (You did realise that you can withdraw net interest from a TESSA as long as you leave intact the capital and the amount of interest which represents the tax-free element? Many people find this a useful source of tax-free income. Your bank or other TESSA-holder should be able to advise you.)

Shares Investment Accounts: use these for shares in companies listed on the Stock Exchange, and for other investments whose prices are listed daily in the financial pages of newspapers and which pay (or are expected eventually to pay) more or less regular dividends: preference shares and debentures; unit and investment trust holdings; government securities ('Gilts'). More speculative investments such as options and futures belong in this category, too. For more about Investment Accounts, see Chapter Seven.

Other Asset Accounts: use these for

● holdings of a fixed, unchanging value such as the Guaranteed Income Bonds sold by insurance companies; National Savings Income Bonds; Premium Bonds.

● investments which do not yield any income until they mature: National Savings Certificates and Capital Bonds; with-profits insurance policies; many of the guaranteed bonds offered by insurance companies; your investments in Business Expansion Schemes ('BESs'). (The Chancellor of the Exchequer has announced that there will be no more BESs after the end of 1993.)

- real estate.

- loans you may have made, perhaps to a member of your family;

- any other property you want to include: your car, perhaps; a valuable collection. You can include under this heading a valuation of all your furniture and other movable property if you think it's worth the trouble.

Liabilities

Your main asset is quite likely to be your house, and your main liability is probably your mortgage. You may also have other borrowings, such as a car loan or some hire purchase agreements. Identifying liabilities is lamentably easy, although finding out exactly how much you owe can be strangely difficult. If you decide to put all your assets in asset accounts, you will have to tell *Quicken* about the corresponding liabilities in order to complete the picture.

An overdrawn bank account, whether the overdraft was authorised by the bank or not, is also a loan and therefore a liability. But the easiest way to handle that in *Quicken* is to treat it as a current/deposit account. *Quicken* 'knows' when the account is overdrawn and will include it as a liability in your Net Worth reports.

You set up an asset or liability account in the way already familiar: from the Main Menu, choose Select Account. From the account list, choose the item at the top, '<New Account>'. You will see that 'Other Asset' and 'Other Liability' are among the six types of account you can now choose from.

Liabilities will be discussed shortly. We'll start with asset accounts. Both should be considered together, however. If you decide that liability accounting is unnecessarily complicated for your purposes, you should leave some assets out of your *Quicken* data as well – the ones that directly correspond to liabilities.

Creating Asset Accounts

Before you begin, you will probably have given some thought to what assets you own, and which of them you want to record in your accounts. Various assets can be lumped together in one account, if you like, but there is one important factor to remember: tax.

● Be sure that assets relevant to your tax returns are kept separate from those that are tax-free. For example, for most people there will be no Capital Gains Tax payable when they sell the house they live in. But if you own a second home, or houses for rent, any increase in their value over the purchase price will be subject to Capital Gains Tax when you come to sell. So keep them in separate Asset Accounts.

● Married couples need to distinguish between assets they own jointly and those which are held in the sole name of one or the other partner. That is because married women are now taxed separately from their husbands. You may not pay much attention in the daily management of your finances to the question of whose name or names are on the title deeds. But the tax man cares. You can still put similar assets in one asset account and distinguish among them by the use of Classes, if you like. You could have one Class called 'His', one called 'Hers', and one called 'Ours'.

National Savings Certificates are completely free of tax. If you own various certificates issued by the government at different times, you might want to gather them conveniently together in one asset account. The income from National Savings Capital Bonds and Income Bonds, however, is taxable, although it is paid to you in full without the deduction of any tax. So they should be in a separate Asset Account from Savings Certificates.

To set up your first Asset Account, choose 'Other Asset' from the Set Up New Account window. Put £0.00 for the opening balance. You will see that the columns to the right of the Transaction Register of an Asset Account are headed

'Decrease', 'Increase' and 'Balance' as well as the familiar 'C' which you can mark with an asterisk when an asset is finally disposed of.

Print/Acct Edit Shortcuts Reports Activities F1-Help

DATE	REF	DESCRIPTION · MEMO · CATEGORY	DECREASE	C	INCREASE	BALANCE
		BEGINNING				
1/ 9 1992		Opening Balance [Home]			152,879 00	152,879 00
23/ 9 1992		EasyBrick Building Co. [Visa]			495 67	153,374 67
16/ 3 1993	Memo: Cat:					

Home (Alt+letter accesses menu)
Esc-Main Menu Ctrl◄┘ Record Ending Balance: £153,374.67

Fig. 6.1. An Asset Account

To start the account off, enter a separate transaction for the value of each asset. You will probably want to use today's date and a current valuation, but in some cases you may prefer an historic date and the actual price you paid for the asset. In the Category field, put the name of the asset account itself (called a 'self-transfer') and one or more Classes, if you like. For example, if you set up an asset account called Treasure for valuable personal possessions of different sorts, the entry in the Category field could be something like 'Treasure/Jewellry/Hers' or 'Treasure/Antiques/Ours'. Use the Memo field to describe the item specifically: 'sapphire earrings' or 'Regency side table'. When all the assets you want to include have been listed, you can double back and delete the £0.00 opening balance.

Valuing Assets

Some assets (Premium Bonds, National Savings Income Bonds) will never change in value. For the others, you should plan to update the value regularly. Once a year is a sensible target.

You can get a leaflet from the Post Office showing the current value of your National Savings Certificates. The redemption value increases annually on the anniversary of the day you bought them. Your National Savings Capital Bonds also increase annually: you will receive an a Statement of Value without having to ask for it. Your insurance company should send you an annual statement showing the current value of your guaranteed bonds.

Setting a value on property which does not have a fixed, cashable value is much more difficult. It is a principle of accounting, and a good general rule of life as well, to err on the side of caution. The insurance value of the things you own is likely to be appreciably higher than their asset value – because you are insuring against the possibility of having to replace them, whereas the asset value is only what the market would pay you if you tried to sell.

You can probably value your house fairly accurately by paying attention to the selling prices of similar houses in your neighbourhood. Bear in mind that the 'selling price' is very often substantially different from the 'asking price'. In hard times, the owner may have to accept a good deal less than hoped for. When real estate prices are booming, competitive bidders may drive the selling price higher than the asking price. Or you could use your Council Tax banding as a basis for a valuation.

You can value your car informally by asking at the garage where you have it serviced, or by looking up the make and year in publications devoted to the subject. If you do, you will find a range of values. It would be prudent to pick one for yourself towards the bottom of the range. If you ask at the garage, remember that the trade-in of your car value will be higher than the asset value, which represents only what you could hope to get for your car in cash.

If you have a valuable collection of any sort, you probably know of reference books which will give you at least a rough idea of current values. If your collection is so precious that you have it regularly valued for insurance purposes, ask the valuer for an estimate of the asset value as well. If you are watching current auction prices as a guide, remember that the seller does not get the entire 'hammer price' at an auction. The auctioneer deducts a certain percentage, and there may be other charges connected with the sale as well.

When you have decided on an up-to-date valuation of an asset, you need to enter it in *Quicken*. Open the Transaction Register of the Asset Account. If you have only one asset in the account, revaluation is simplicity itself. From the Transaction Register, press `[Alt]-[A]` for the Activities menu on the toolbar. Choose Update Account Balance. Type in the new valuation and press `[Enter]`. *Quicken* will create an adjustment transaction for the amount of the difference.

If you have put several assets together in one Asset Account, you will have to enter the adjustment transaction yourself. Accept today's date unless you have some reason for wanting to date the valuation otherwise. You may want to fill in the Description or Memo field with the name, perhaps in brackets, of the particular asset you are re-valuing. That is because as far as *Quicken* is concerned, the increase or decrease in value you are about to record applies to the whole account; but you will want to monitor the values of the separate assets in the account individually.

In the Decrease or Increase columns, as appropriate, be sure to put only the **difference** between the last valuation and the current one, not the whole new value. Remember that there is no need to burden yourself with any arithmetic – the *Quicken* calculator will do it for you, and if your cursor is in the Decrease or the Increase column when you invoke the calculator, you can use `[F9]` to paste the result into the Transaction Register.

Transfers from Asset Accounts

As well as entering an annual valuation, you will occasionally want to make transfers to or from an Asset Account. If you buy a new Rembrandt for your private picture gallery, enter the cheque in the Transaction Register of the account you took the money from, and designate it as a transfer to the appropriate asset account. You'll probably want to put the name of your new picture in the Description or Memo field. You cannot assign a transfer of funds between accounts to an income or an expense category, but you can designate a Class for transfers. So when you pay for your Rembrandt from your current account and transfer it to your asset account called Treasure, designate the transfer as 'Treasure/Pictures/His', or whatever seems appropriate.

Use the same approach when you make improvements to a house you own, other than the one you live in. Enter the cheque in the Transaction Register of the account you took the money from, but designate it as a transfer to the Asset Account which includes the house, rather than assigning it to an expense category. Houses other than your main residence are liable to Capital Gains Tax when you sell, but improvements you have made may count as part of the cost of the house and thus reduce your tax liability. The expense of maintaining property is not relevant here, and should not be transferred to an asset account. You may be able to set maintenance expenses off against your rental income, however, if you own a house which is let to tenants. See Chapter Nine on the business uses of *Quicken*.

When an asset matures or is sold, mark the asset itself with an asterisk in the column headed 'C' in the Transaction Register of the Asset Account. That lets *Quicken* know that the asset is no longer current. If you have recorded any increases or decreases in the value of that asset, you will need to mark them, too. If necessary, enter a final increase or decrease (and mark it with an asterisk at once) so that the total value of the asset as recorded in the account is equal to the amount you got for it. Then enter in the Asset Account a transfer of that amount to the account where you deposited the money you received. Again, mark the transfer in the Transaction Register of the asset account with an asterisk.

The process of transferring money out of an Asset Account in *Quicken* can help you watch for the maturity date of Savings Certificates. Beyond that date, which is clearly stated on the certificate, you will continue to be credited with tax- free interest but at a much reduced rate; and the government will not remind you when repayment is due.

So when your annual valuation reveals that the certificates have less than a year to go, let *Quicken* remind you instead.

Enter in your Asset Account the final transfer of the redemption value of the certificates to the account where you plan to put the money. Date the transaction in advance to the date your repayment is due. The sight from time to time of that nice sum below the double line in the account which is looking forward to the money, and the plump 'Closing Balance' (which will include the repayment) in the lower right-hand corner of the screen, will serve to ensure that you send the certificates in for repayment at the right time.

Or if you're really worried about remembering, you could 'write' a silly cheque of some sort from the Write Cheques option on *Quicken*'s Main Menu, date it for when the certificates are due to mature, and let Billminder remind you, starting up to 30 days in advance of the redemption date, whenever you switch your computer on. Delete the silly cheque, of course, once you have actually redeemed the Savings Certificates. See the section on the Billminder in Chapter Five.

Or if you have a Shares Investment account, you could enter a Reminder in the register. See Chapter Seven.

Once you start making transfers between asset or liability accounts and your other, everyday accounts, you will need to take a little extra care with reports to make sure that they are telling you what you want to know. See the section on reports at the end of this chapter.

If you have assets which pay you an income, such as National Savings Income Bonds or a house you own and rent out, enter the income in the account where you actually put it. Assign it to an appropriate income category. Do not make any entry concerning the income in the asset account. Entries in an asset account are only for events which affect the value of the asset. Your Premium Bond wins should also be treated in this way, but they are completely tax-free so you will need to remember to assign them to an income category which is not designated 'tax-related'.

Creating a Liability Account

You may be somewhat surprised to learn how less-than-easy it is to discover exactly what your liabilities are. You know how much you borrowed when you bought your house; you certainly know how much you are paying the bank or the building society every month in repayment. But do you know how much you still owe? The effort of finding out may be the final straw which persuades you to give up the idea of liability accounting.

If, however, you are still determined to include liability accounts, *Quicken* can be of some help.

There are loans, such as bank overdrafts and mortgages, which may be subject to change when interest rates go up or down. And there are others, bank loans or hire-purchase contracts, for which you know at the beginning exactly how many payments you have to make and how much each one will be. We'll start with those.

The Loan Calculator

From the Transaction Register of any account, press `[Alt]-[A]` for the Activities menu on the toolbar. Choose Loan Calculator from the Activities menu. You will see a window in which you can fill in four items relevant to a loan: the Principal, the Annual Interest Rate, Total Years, and Periods per Year. The principal, of course, is the amount the item actually cost in the shop, if this is a hire-purchase agreement; or the full amount of cash you received, if this is a bank loan. You will have agreed the total number of years the loan is to last. If the lender quotes more than one interest rate, the one to use here is the 'APR', the Annual Percentage Rate. Lenders are required by law to state it. You will almost certainly be paying the loan off by monthly installments, so Periods per Year will be 12.

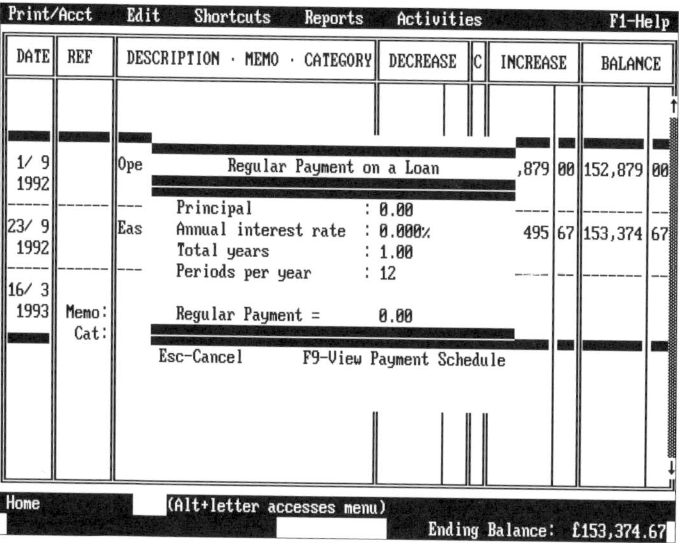

Fig. 6.2. The Loan Calculator

When you have filled in these four fields, press `[Tab]`. *Quicken* will calculate how much each of your regular payments should be. You undoubtedly know the answer already.

If *Quicken*'s answer is markedly different from what you expected, you should pursue the matter with the shop or with your bank. You may have agreed to pay more interest than you realised.

Assuming all is well, press `[F9]` to view the Approximate Payment Schedule. *Quicken* will show you, for each of your payments until the end of the loan period, how much is principal and how much is interest. You will have to return to this window regularly so that you can enter each payment correctly.

The payments will probably be made by Standing Order from one of your accounts. Set up the Standing Order as described in Chapter Two so that *Quicken* can enter the payments in the Transaction Register automatically when they fall due. You have a choice at this point as to how you want to finish things off:

● The easier and less professional way, involving no transfers between accounts, is to assign the whole payment to an expense category. Every month when the payment is made, check with the Approximate Payment Schedule to see how much of the payment was principal. Open the liability account in which you keep the loan, and enter the amount of principal in the Decrease column. If you have more than one loan in the same liability account, use a Class or just a note in the Description or Memo field to remind yourself which one this payment applies to.

● The harder and more accurate alternative choice is to assign the monthly payment, when you are setting up the Standing Order, to an expense category called 'Interest'. To track your expenditure even more closely, make the 'Interest' Category into a subcategory. Interest on a car loan could become a subcategory of the expense category called Motor, for example.

When the monthly payment is made, look up the Approximate Payment Schedule as before to find out how much of the payment was principal. Then split the transaction, leaving the interest element in the interest expense category and designating the rest as a transfer to the liability account containing the loan. Use a Description, Memo or Class, as before, to identify the particular loan if necessary. Unfortunately you cannot set up the Standing Order to split the transaction for you automatically, because the amount of principal and interest will be different every month.

What if you took out the loan some time before you started using *Quicken*, and now want to enter it in a liability account?

Start out in the same way. Set up a Standing Order for the monthly payments. Consult the Loan Calculator, entering the full amount of the original borrowing, the interest rate you agreed to pay, and the number of payments you agreed to make. *Quicken* will tell you, as before, what your monthly payments are. If the figure is not at least approximately right, you will have to try to figure out where you have gone wrong in filling in the details of the loan.

Unfortunately, you cannot simply fill in the figure you certainly know, namely 'Regular Payment', and let *Quicken* work out the interest rate. But it's very easy to keep trying different figures for the interest rate until the Regular Payment approximates the truth. When *Quicken*'s figure for the payments coincides with reality, press `[F9]` to see the Approximate Payment Schedule.

Next, decide how many payments you have already made. Scan down the 'Pmt' (Payment) column until you reach that number. Note the figure given for 'Balance'. That's how much you still owe. Return to the Transaction Register of your liability account. Enter a transaction, using today's date and putting something like 'Amount paid to date' in the description column. With the cursor in the 'Decrease' column, press `[Ctrl]-[O]` to summon the *Quicken* calculator. Now subtract the balance – the amount you noted down from the Approximate Payment Schedule window – from the amount of the original loan. Press `[F9]` to paste the answer into the transaction register. Press `[Ctrl]-[Enter]` to tell *Quicken* to accept the transaction.

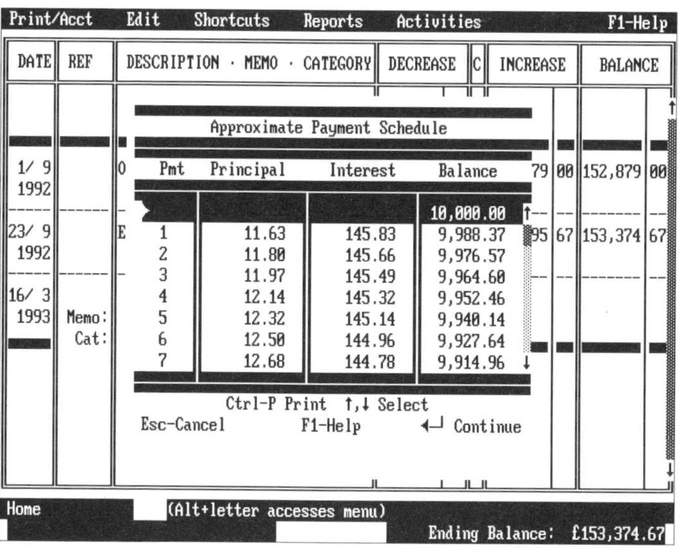

Fig. 6.3. Approximate Payment Schedule

From here on out, you proceed as for a new loan, deciding whether you are just going to assign the payments to an expense category and make a separate entry in the liability account of the amount of principal repaid; or whether you will conscientiously transfer the amount of principal repaid each time from the source account to the liability account.

Mortgages

The complications here are a lot worse, and, again, it's not *Quicken*'s fault.

To begin with, a number of charges may have been added to your loan such as a valuation fee, a conveyancer's fee, a mortgage indemnity premium and/or a mortgage discharge fee. Furthermore, some lenders regard the outstanding principal as fixed for a calendar year, so that although each of your payments includes both principal and interest, you do not get credit for the principal repaid until the end of the year. The effect of such sleights-of-hand is to increase the real interest rate you are paying, and to make it more difficult to use *Quicken*'s Loan Calculator to figure out exactly what is going on.

The best course if you are determined to forge ahead is probably to set up a liability account containing the amount you borrowed in the first place, plus any charges you know about. Once a year, preferably in January, make the lender tell you how much principal is outstanding. You can be sure that the lender's computer records that amount clearly even if no one seems very keen to tell you. When you have succeeded in finding out, from the Transaction Register of your mortgage liability account, choose Update Account Balance from the Activities menu on the toolbar. Type in the new principal amount. *Quicken* will adjust the balance in your liability account. And you will be horrified in the early years of a mortgage to discover how little progress you are making: that can be guaranteed.

On this system, you will treat your actual mortgage payments as an expense and not record any transfers into the liability account.

Endowment Mortgages

If you have an endowment mortgage, things are simpler in one sense: the entire amount of the mortgage remains outstanding for the entire life of the mortgage. So you can set up your mortgage liability account and leave it strictly alone thereafter, until the happy moment when the entire debt is repaid. You will be paying interest on the loan, of course, and that interest will vary from time to time. Create an expense category for mortgage interest but do not transfer any of the payments to the liability account.

You will also, under this system, have an endowment insurance policy. You pay monthly premiums (which should never change) to the insurance company, and at the end of the term you will receive the full amount owed on the mortgage. Life insurance is included, so the mortgage would be paid off if you should die before the end of the term. And many such endowment policies are 'with profits', meaning that you should get some cash for yourself at the end of the mortgage. The actual amount will depend on how well the insurance company has done at investing your money in the mean time.

You will probably have realised by now that the endowment policy constitutes an asset. The great difficulty is, how to value it? The difficulty is compounded by the fact that if you cash it in before it has run its full term you are likely to get a poor return.

You could:

- treat all your premiums as transfers of value to the endowment policy asset account. For the first few years – possibly five years or more – this system will overstate the value of the policy. Later on, however, the policy should be worth more than the accumulated premiums, so you will then be understating its value.

- divide the total amount of the mortgage loan by the total number of years the loan and the policy are to run, and credit that amount to the endowment policy asset account each year. Regard your premiums as an expense and do not try to transfer value between accounts.

● use the annual statements you receive from the insurance company as a basis for valuing the asset, or as a means to make adjustments to either of the other two methods.

Assets and Liabilities in Reports

If you adopt any system of asset or liability accounting (or both, of course) which involves transfers to or from any of your current, deposit or cash accounts, you will have to be make sure that they are correctly listed in your reports.

With a report on-screen, `[Alt]-[L]` will take you to the Layout Menu. If you choose Other Options from that menu, you will see a window in which you can specify how you want your reports to deal with transfers. You can 'Include All', 'Exclude All' or include 'External Transfers Only'. The third choice is the one you are most likely to want – if you 'Include All', your report will show transfers from your deposit account to your current account, or from your current account to cash – transfers which have no effect on your actual financial position. The choice of 'External Transfers Only' will ensure that transfers to and from your asset and liability accounts are included, but not the others.

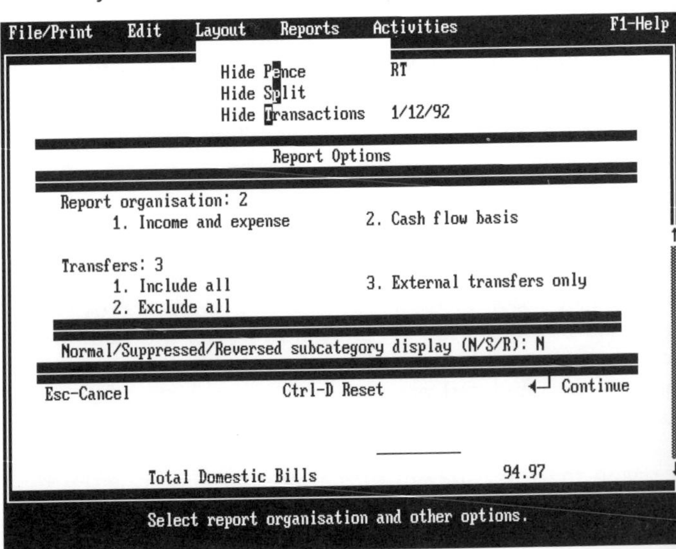

Fig. 6.4. Transfers between Accounts

When you are setting up a budget, you can similarly choose whether or not to include transfers. If you have set up a liability account which receives a regular transfer of funds from some other account as you pay off the debt, you will certainly want to include those payments in your budgeting. From the budget screen, press `[Alt]-[E]` for the Edit menu on the toolbar, and choose Budget Transfers from that menu. You can turn transfers off again by repeating the process.

There may be times, however, when you want to exclude asset and liability account transfers from a report. You may not want the repayment of your National Savings Certificates to figure in a Cash Flow Report, for instance. In that case, filter the report to exclude the asset account where the Savings Certificates were listed. See Chapter Four for more on reports and how to filter them.

CHAPTER

Shares investment accounts

FEATURING

- Setting up an investment account
- Investment graphs and reports

Computer budget programs with the ability to monitor a portfolio of stockmarket investments have been available in America for some years. But in late 1992 *Quicken* broke new ground in Britain by including this feature in a domestic budget program. Whether your portfolio forms a major part of your wealth or consists of a handful of BT shares bravely acquired on privatisation, you will want to set up a Shares Investment Account and reap the advantages of having all your financial affairs under one electronic roof.

Shares Investment Accounts

Quicken's Shares Investment Accounts are intended for savers whose shareholdings are part of a long-term savings plan. If you speculate on the movement of share prices, perhaps by buying or selling options, you should take the advice of your stockbroker about computer software to monitor events. Your profits or losses on such transactions can be recorded in *Quicken*. You may want to keep them separate from your Shares Investment account by assigning them to an income category such as Dealing Profits and entering them directly in a bank account. (An income category can include losses as well as gains.) But options can equally well be listed in a Shares Investment account if you prefer.

See Chapter Six, *Asset and Liability Accounts*, for some detailed suggestions on how to classify your savings and investments and distribute them among the various types of account available in *Quicken*. A Shares Investment Account is, essentially, for holdings whose price fluctuations are listed daily in the financial press.

British investors usually (not always) hold securities in their own name and receive dividends directly as a cheque in the post or a payment into a bank account. A stockbroker gives advice and may have responsibility for monitoring a portfolio and making investment suggestions. The stockbroker will also make the actual sale or purchase of securities and charge a commission for doing so.

American investors often maintain an account with a stockbroking firm which holds all securities in its name, and collects the dividends. The investor receives a monthly statement showing the current value of the securities and the amount of accumulated cash from the dividends, very like a bank statement. If you had an account with the famous stockbroking firm of Merrill Lynch, Pierce, Fenner & Smith in New York, you could have a chequebook and credit card allowing you to draw on your dividend income directly, and the income you didn't draw would itself earn interest.

The *Quicken* system shadows an arrangement like that. And who knows? perhaps one day more stockmarket dealings in this country will be done that way. Meanwhile the *Quicken* setup is easy enough to adapt to the British way of doing things.

Creating Share Investment Accounts

● If you have shares in relatively few separate companies or unit trusts – up to about a dozen, let us say – it might be best to put each one in a separate account. Think of the accounts as separate folders in which you keep your investment papers, or separate sections of a ring binder.

● As with assets (see Chapter Six) it is important for tax purposes to separate securities held in a couple's joint name from those held in the sole name of either one. It is wisest to put them in separate accounts from the beginning, although you could construct a system using *Quicken*'s Classes to sort the dividends out. The section in Chapter Eight about using *Quicken* to help prepare your tax return has more on this subject.

● If you hold shares in a PEP (Personal Equity Plan), put them together in one account, a separate account for each PEP if you have several. The rewards of a PEP are completely tax free, both the dividends and the capital gains.

● If you do have an American-type account with a stockbroker, you will want to put those shares together in one *Quicken* account.

● If you have a sizeable portfolio, with too many individual holdings to make it convenient to have a separate account for each one, you might like to have separate accounts for different types of investment: government securities ('Gilts') in one, ordinary shares in another, investment trusts in another, unit trusts in another. The reason for doing it that way is more than general tidiness – it helps with the updating of prices.

Although *Quicken* is quite clever about foreign currencies in other respects – see Chapter Five – you cannot have a Shares Investment Account in anything other than your home currency. If your financial sophistication rises to the point of owning shares in Tokyo, Paris or New York, you will have to keep them in a separate *Quicken* file. See Chapter Ten, *Nuts and Bolts*, for how to do that.

When you have made the necessary decisions about how to arrange things, the procedure for actually opening a Shares Investment Account is the familiar one. From the Main Menu, choose Select Account; from the list of your accounts, choose New Account>, at the top of the list. From the Set Up New Account window, choose 6, Shares Investment.

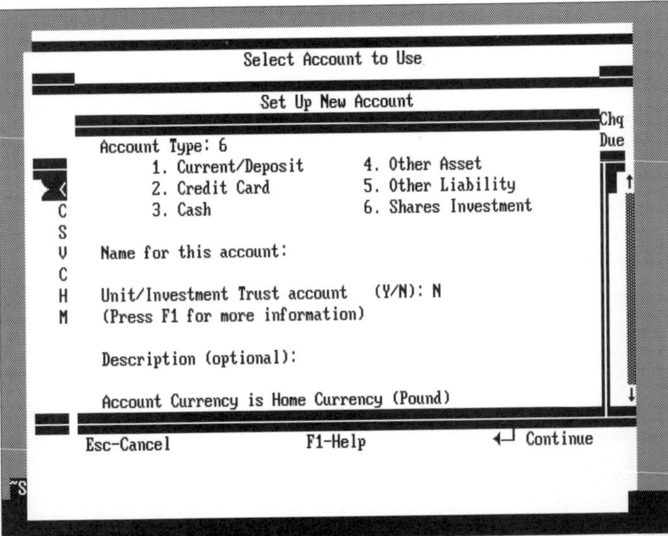

Fig. 7.1. Setting up a Share Account

Two Types of Share Account

Quicken offers two types of Shares Investment account. A unit/investment trust account is for one security only, and cannot have a cash balance. A normal Shares Investment account can include more than one security, and can have a cash balance.

As already explained, you probably won't be interested in a cash balance. Assuming that you have decided to put each of your stockmarket holdings in a separate account, there is something to be said for using *Quicken*'s unit/investment trust type of account for the purpose, even for ordinary shares in individual companies. This is especially true if you often buy more shares (or sell a few) in a holding, perhaps because you sometimes take shares in lieu of a dividend.

The unit/investment trust type of account shows your balance in terms of the number of shares held, rather than as a cash balance. Of course there is a way to get that total if you list your shares in the other type of Shares Investment account, but you might consider it an advantage to be able to check at a glance to see how many shares you currently hold.

The procedure from here is much the same whichever type of account you choose. You are going to provide the details about the holding or holdings in this particular account. (In what follows, a 'share' can mean a unit in a unit trust as well as an ordinary share in a company or in an investment trust.) As so often, *Quicken* is relaxed at this important point as to what sort of information you need to provide.

Adding New Shares

When you open the Transaction Register of your Shares Investment account for the first time, a window will pop open:

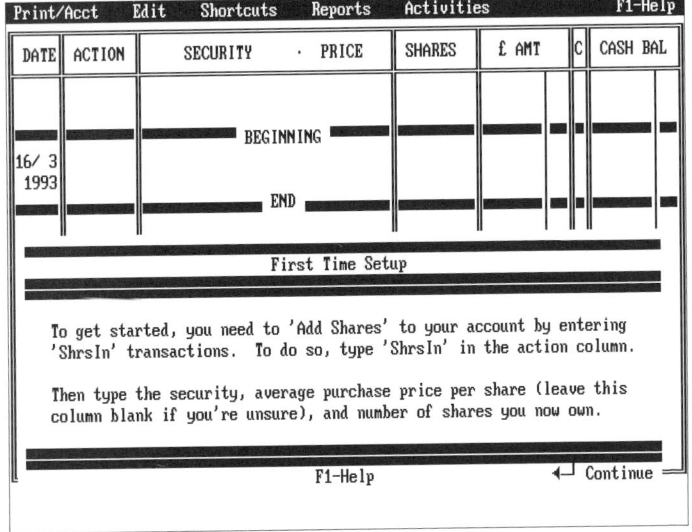

Print/Acct Edit Shortcuts Reports Activities F1-Help
DATE ACTION SECURITY · PRICE SHARES £ AMT C CASH BAL
BEGINNING
16/ 3 1993
END
First Time Setup
To get started, you need to 'Add Shares' to your account by entering 'ShrsIn' transactions. To do so, type 'ShrsIn' in the action column.
Then type the security, average purchase price per share (leave this column blank if you're unsure), and number of shares you now own.
F1-Help
Continue

Fig. 7.2. First - Time Data Entry

You will have to enter information about your shareholdings. **Date:** If all your paper work is in a state of immaculate order, you can put here the date when you originally bought the share. Or if you at least have records for the recent past, you can put the date of the start of the current tax year, last April 6. Or you can put today's date and resolve (or not) to go back and fill in historical data later.

This date relates to the optional first valuation you provide for the holding. *Quicken* will use that valuation, if provided, as a 'cost basis' to calculate your capital gains or losses. Even if you can't find the original papers, perhaps because you inherited the shares from your Aunt Agnes sometime before the dawn of history, you might choose to put the date of an old valuation of the holding which you happen to have recorded, just to provide *Quicken* with a cost basis.

Action: When you are starting off a new investment account, you will put 'ShrsIn' here, meaning 'Shares In'. That allows you to tell *Quicken* about your investments without having to transfer money from another account to 'pay' for them.

Security: Type the name of the share, 'BT' or 'Abbey Ethical Growth' or 'Treasury 7 1/4% 1998' or whatever it may be. It is important for analysis purposes in the future that *Quicken* always understands exactly which share you mean. For this reason the program maintains a list of shares rather like the list of income and expense categories you are already familiar with. When you type a name it doesn't recognise – and it won't recognise anything, the first time you type it – a window will appear saying 'Security Not Found'. You then choose whether to add your security to the list or pick the one you really meant from the list.

If you choose to add your new share to the list, you will see the Set Up Security window. The name you just typed into the account register has already been filled in.

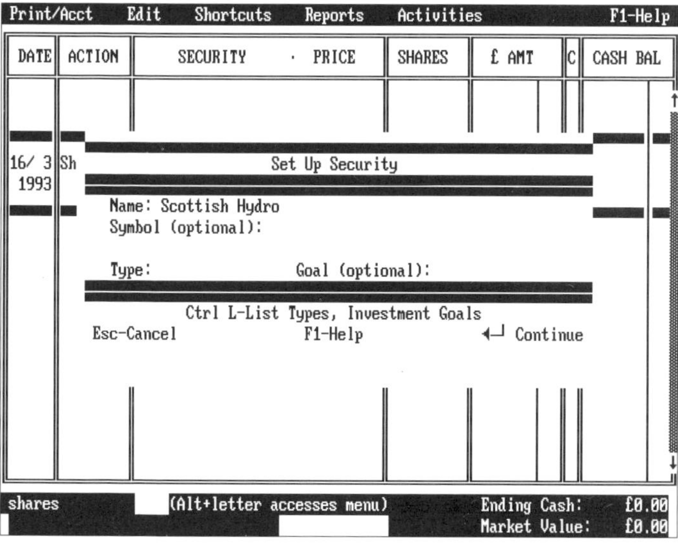

Fig. 7.3 'Set Up Security' window

You can specify a symbol if you like. That can be useful if you want to import a price history for your share, or to distinguish between different lots of the same share.

Next, you must specify a Type for your share. *Quicken* supplies a list of suggested Types such as 'Bond', 'Gilt',

'Shares' and 'Unit/Investment Trust.' Fortunately, you do not have to accept any of the suggestions. DON'T. Here's why:

Stock Market Sectors

American newspapers list all the shares on the New York Stock Exchange in alphabetical order from A to Z. British newspapers list them alphabetically by sectors – Banks, Breweries, Building Shares and so on – with the individual companies alphabetically within each sector. When you are updating the prices of your shares from a newspaper, *Quicken* will present them to you alphabetically by **Type.**

So unless you have very few shares, or don't mind waving the newspaper around a lot, you must replace *Quicken*'s Types with sectors, as listed in your own newspaper. Each newspaper has its own classification of shares, no two quite the same. *Quicken* allows you only 15 Types. You may have to make judicious use of 'Miscellaneous' if you have a large portfolio.

This is the reason for putting your Gilts and your Unit Trusts in a separate *Quicken* account from your ordinary shares. All newspapers put Gilts and Unit Trusts in separate lists, often on a separate page from ordinary shares. You don't want Gilts to pop up in between Food Retailing and Health and Household when you are trying to update prices.

From the Set Up Security window, then, with your cursor in the Type field, press `[Ctrl]-[L]` to see *Quicken*'s list of Types.

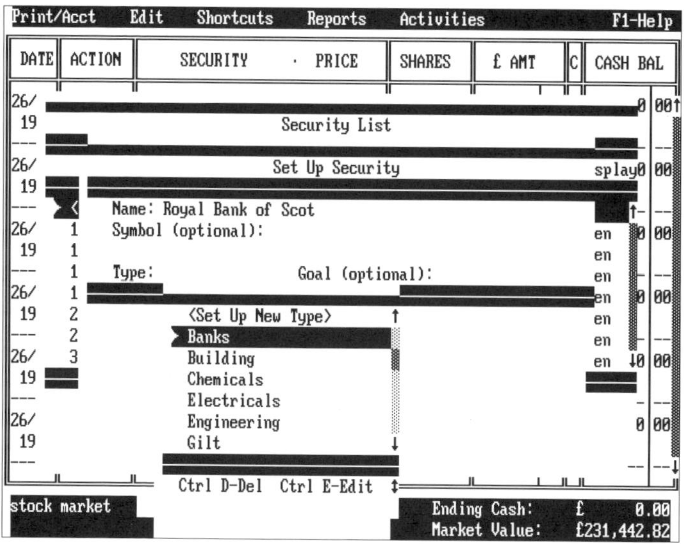

Fig. 7.4 Replacing Types with Sectors

If you're going to need all 15 Types for your own portfolio, delete *Quicken*'s suggestions by moving the highlight to each one and pressing **[Alt]-[D]**. Then choose <Set Up New Type> from the top of the list.

The Set Up Security Type window needs only two pieces of information. In the 'Type' field, put the name of a sector you want to use. You can then choose whether you want the price display for your sector in decimals or fractions. Choose decimals.

Here's why: the prices of American shares, for some curious reason, are listed in dollars and fractions of a dollar – '46 1/4' is bad enough, instead of '$46.25', but you will also find '46 3/8'. *Quicken* has been set up to cope with that.

British share prices are listed in pence so the problem doesn't often arise. When it does, the fraction is an easy one, 1/2 or possibly 1/4.

On the other hand, the prices of government securities,

'Gilts', do involve fractions here in Britain. But *Quicken* will only print fractions which are multiples of 1/2 or 1/8, like the fractions in American share prices. British Gilt prices can have fractions as awful as '27/32'. *Quicken* can understand a fraction like that when you type it in from your newspaper (thank goodness), but it will express it as a decimal. So you might as well choose decimals in the first place for everything.

The final piece of information requested by the Set Up Security window is 'Goal'. This is optional. 'Growth', 'Income', and 'High Risk' are among the suggested goals. You may find this too much to think about on the day you set up your investment accounts for the first time. You can always come back and fill in some goals later on. They provide another, possibly a very useful, way to arrange shares for analysis.

The First Transactions

Now press `[Enter]`. Your new share is on the list, and you are back in the Shares Investment account register. The share list will be common to all your investment accounts. You may have shares in the same company in more than one account – perhaps because some of your shares are in a PEP while others are owned outright; or because you and your wife or husband each own shares in the same company in your individual names. *Quicken* understands. And when you update prices, you need provide the new price only once. *Quicken* will update all the accounts that contain that share.

DATE	ACTION	SECURITY · PRICE	SHARES	£ AMT	C	CASH BAL
		BEGINNING				
16/ 3 1993	ShrsIn	Abbey National ·374	400	1,496 00		0 00
16/ 3 1993	ShrsIn	Guinness ·523	2,140	11,192 20		0 00
16/ 3 1993	ShrsIn	Blue Circle ·171	3,411	5,832 81		0 00
16/ 3 1993	ShrsIn	BOC ·755	307	2,317 85		0 00
16/ 3 1993						
		END				

Print/Acct Edit Shortcuts Reports Activities F1-Help

shares (Alt+letter accesses menu) Ending Cash: £ 0.00
Esc-Main Menu Ctrl◄┘ Record Market Value: £20,838.86

Fig. 7.5 A Shares Investment Account

There is a little more information to enter in the register: 'Price', 'Shares', and '£ Amt'. 'Shares' means 'number of shares', and that is the only information *Quicken* insists on here. You can leave 'Price' and '£ Amt' blank but you might as well put something – see below for what to put – so that *Quicken* has a cost basis for your shares.

The three items are connected – the Pound Amount equals the Price times the Number of Shares. *Quicken* understands that, so you need to fill in only the number of shares and either the Price or the Pound Amount. *Quicken* will calculate the missing number.

● If you have all the paper work handy and want to put the full history of your shareholding into *Quicken*, you will have started by typing in the date on which you bought the shares. Now, using your stockbroker's bill to provide the information you need, skip Price and type in the total amount you paid for the shares, including the stockbroker's commission and any other charges, in the Pound Amount column. *Quicken* will use this as the cost basis for calculating your future profits (or losses).

● *Quicken* does not cater for buying shares by installments. If the share is a privatisation and if you have records which tell you exactly how much you paid and when, put only the amount of the first installment here and use the technique described under Special Situations at the end of this chapter to enter the subsequent payments. Otherwise put the full amount you have paid so far for the Pound Amount. There will be no charges to add. The date should be the date of the first installment.

● If you have entered last April 6 as the date because you intend to provide complete data for the current tax year, type in the Price of the share as listed in the newspaper on or around April 6. Then *Quicken* will calculate your capital gains (and losses) for the current tax year, and for the future starting from last April 6.

● If you started off with the date of an old valuation, put that valuation here, either as Price or as Pound Amount.

● And if you're starting from now, type in the Price from today's newspaper.

> *Quicken* expects the price to be expressed in pence, that is, in hundredths of a pound, as is normal in this country. If you have set up a file for a foreign share portfolio with some other currency than sterling as the 'home currency', you can change that: choose Set Preferences from the Main Menu; choose Country Settings from the Set Preferences menu. Shares on the New York Stock Exchange, for example, are priced in dollars, not pennies.
> You will have to fudge things slightly with your Gilts. For these, the newspapers list the value of £100 'par value' of the security. That's a bit confusing, and not just for *Quicken*.
>
> Let's say you bought £100 par value of Treasury 7 1/4% 1998 in March, 1993. You would have paid about £103 for it, plus dealing costs. Tell *Quicken* you have 100 'shares' of 7 1/4% Treasury 1998. Put the actual amount of the cheque you wrote as the Pound Amount – it will have been somewhat more than £103 because of costs. Then in the future when you're updating the price, type it in like any other price, as if it were expressed in pence: 103. It'll come out right, honest.

If you have adopted the one-account-per-share option, you will now need to double back and open a new account for the next share. If you have opened a normal Shares Investment Account and want to add more shares, repeat the process you have just gone through.

Since *Quicken* allows you to alter a Transaction Register, you can later go back and improve the information you originally supplied. Perhaps after you have set up your Shares Investment portfolio, you will look out the original stockbroker's accounts and want to provide a fully accurate cost basis for some or all of your holdings.

Now that you have set up one or more Shares Investment Accounts, there are various things you might want to do:

- Add the name of a share you don't own, or of an index, to the Security List, so that you can track its performance.
- Record dividends, sales, purchases, and other events in your account or accounts.
- Update the prices of all your shares.
- Look at *Quicken*'s investment reports to see how you are getting on.
- Look at performance graphs for your shares and perhaps measure them against a stock market index.

Tracking Shares You Don't Own

Easy. From the Transaction Register of your Shares Investment account, press `[Ctrl]-[Y]` for the Securities List. Choose New Security from the top of the list. Add the share or index in the usual way. The Financial Times 100-share index, known as the 'FT-SE-100' or the 'Footsie', is a good index to use. If you still have a Type available out of the 15 you are allowed, assign it to a Type called 'Index'. Otherwise it will have to be 'Miscellaneous'.

When you return to the Securities List, move the highlight to your new share or index and press the spacebar until the word in the 'Display' column at the right is 'Always'.

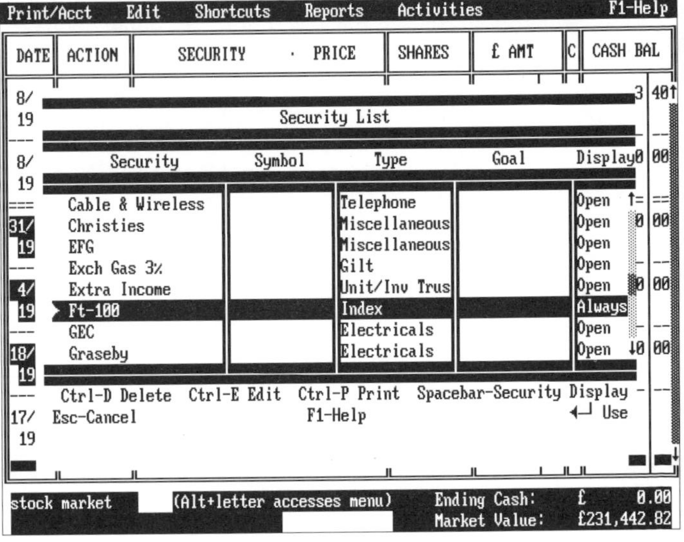

Fig. 7.6 Editing the Security List

The three possibilities for the Display column are 'Always', 'Open', and 'Never'. 'Open' means that the name of the share is displayed on the Update Prices screen only if you own some shares in the company, or have bought or sold put or call options on it, at the date of the update.

Your addition to the Securities List will not appear in your Transaction Register, of course, because you haven't made any transactions which involve it. But you will be able to update its price regularly along with the shares you own and to see graphs comparing its performance with that of your own shares.

Recording Investment Events

Quicken has a predetermined list of possible entries in the 'Action' column of a Shares Investment account. As when you are entering a Category in the Transaction Register of your current account, you need type only enough letters for *Quicken* to be sure which action you mean, and then press `[Enter]`. The program will finish the typing for you.

Some of the actions are not available for a Unit/Investment Trust account, because it has no cash balance. Those actions are marked with an asterisk (*) in the following list.

ShrsIn: You've already used this one, to add shares to an Investment Account without 'paying' for them from any other account.

ShrsOut: Use this one if for any reason you want to remove shares without accounting for them.

***Buy:** You probably won't use this one, as it means that you have bought shares with money which was already in the Shares Investment account.

BuyX: This will be your normal 'action' when you buy shares with money transferred from another account. If you put BuyX, *Quicken* will automatically ask you which account you took the money from to buy the shares, and make an entry in the transaction register of that account. A separate line will appear in the Pound Amount column for you to enter your stockbroker's commission.

***CapGain:** This is for use when you receive cash from a capital gains distribution, and keep the cash in the account.

CapGainX: This is for use when cash from a capital gains distribution is transferred to another account. This action has a special use in the case of a rights issue: see the section 'Special Situations' at the end of this chapter.

***Div:** Receive cash from a dividend and keep it in the Shares Investment account.

DivX: Receive dividend cash into another account. Transfers between accounts usually can't be assigned to income or expense categories, but *Quicken* automatically assigns this one to its own category '_DivInc'.

***IntInc:** Receive cash from interest income and keep it in the account. This one won't be much used, either, as your interest-bearing investments are not usually kept in a Shares Investment account. You might, however, want to classify the money received from your Gilts as '_IntInc' rather than '_DivInc' by using this Action.

***MargInt:** Interest you pay your stockbroker from funds in the account on money you have borrowed for speculative dealings.

***MiscExp:** Miscellaneous investment expenses paid from money in the account. This one is unlikely to be much used.

***MiscInc:** Cash received from miscellaneous income; a nice thought.

Reminder: Important and useful – *Quicken* will remind you of forthcoming investment events, such as an installment due on a privatisation share. See the Special Situations section at the end of this chapter for further details.

***RtrnCap:** Receive cash (and keep it in the account) from 'return of capital'. The most likely use for this one will be when one of your shares is 'bought out' for cash, with or without your approval, but it has a special use when you pay installments on a privatisation share. See under Special Situations at the end of this chapter.

ScrIssue: It sometimes happens that a company splits its shares and issues 'free' new ones to all shareholders. The normal result is that the price of the share on the stock exchange falls to take account of the split, so that the total value of your holding remains more or less unchanged. Use this Action and *Quicken* will be able to adjust the share price on its investment performance graphs so that your share does not appear to have suddenly lost half its value.

ReinvDiv: Use this one if you reinvest in additional shares in the company with money received as a dividend. Unit-holders in many unit trusts elect to receive dividends in this way regularly. It is also increasingly common for companies to offer shareholders the option of taking shares in lieu of dividends.

ReinvInt: This is for reinvesting interest, rather than dividends, in additional shares.

ReinvCG: This is for reinvesting in a security with money from a capital gains distribution. That sounds pretty unlikely, as your best chance of receiving a capital gains distribution is when your company is bought out and there are no more shares to be had.

***Sell:** Sell shares and keep the money in your Shares Investment account.

***SellX:** Sell shares and transfer the money to another account.

***XIn:** Transfer cash into the investment account.

***XOut:** Transfer cash out of the investment account.

Updating Share Prices

You'll want to do this regularly, perhaps once a month. Beginner's enthusiasm and the wish to have some meaningful graphs as soon as possible may inspire you to more frequent updates. It's alright to start with weekly updates and then slacken off later – *Quicken* understands how to do arithmetic involving dates and your graphs will still give a true picture of the situation.

From the Transaction Register of one of your investment accounts, press `[Ctrl]-[U]`. You will see the 'Update Prices and Market Value' screen.

If you have more than one investment account, of either sort, the first thing to do is to check the lower left-hand corner of the screen where *Quicken* tells you which accounts you are about to update. If you have only a few shares, you will want 'All Accounts'. Press `[F9]` to change from the current account to 'All Accounts' if need be. On the other hand, if you have carefully put your ordinary shares in separate accounts from your Gilts or your unit trusts precisely in order to simplify the updating process, you will want to take one account at a time. Press `[F9]` to change back again from 'All Accounts' to the name of the account you were in when you started updating.

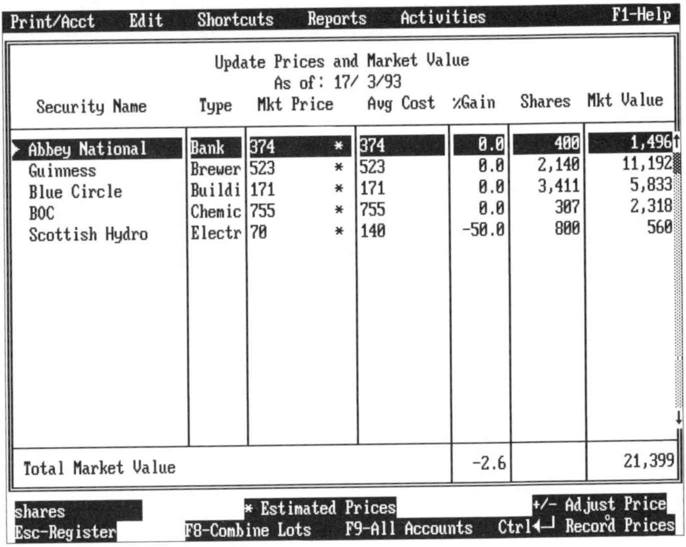

Print/Acct	Edit	Shortcuts	Reports	Activities		F1-Help
Update Prices and Market Value As of: 17/ 3/93						
Security Name	Type	Mkt Price	Avg Cost	%Gain	Shares	Mkt Value
Abbey National	Bank	374 *	374	0.0	400	1,496
Guinness	Brewer	523 *	523	0.0	2,140	11,192
Blue Circle	Buildi	171 *	171	0.0	3,411	5,833
BOC	Chemic	755 *	755	0.0	307	2,318
Scottish Hydro	Electr	70 *	140	-50.0	800	560
Total Market Value				-2.6		21,399

shares | * Estimated Prices | +/- Adjust Price
Esc-Register | F8-Combine Lots | F9-All Accounts | Ctrl↵ Record Prices

Fig. 7.7. Updating Share Prices

You may own different lots of shares in the same company, in the same or different accounts. Perhaps one lot is in your PEP and another is owned directly. You will probably find that *Quicken* has automatically amalgamated the holding on the update screen; if not, press `[F8]` to make it do so. That will save you typing the same price twice.

Now all you have to do is to move the highlight to the price you want to update and type in today's price. Normally, you will start at the top of the list and work down. As you type in each price, you will see the market value of that holding change. When you finish, you will find an updated figure for the 'Total Market Value' at the bottom of your screen.

Press `[F10]` or `[Ctrl]-[Enter]` to record the prices when you are finished.

If you have some old records which you want to incorporate in *Quicken*, press `[Ctrl]-[G]` from the Update Prices and Market Values screen. You will see a window in which you can type in any date. When you do, you will be back at the Update Prices screen with your new date in the heading at the top. Enter the prices in the usual way, and press `F10]` or `[Ctrl]-[Enter]` when you are finished.

To type in a price history for one share only, move the highlight to the share you are interested in and press `[Ctrl]-[H]`. You will see a list of dates and prices for that share. You can add to it or change it as you please.

Investment Reports

Quicken has four special reports available for investment accounts.

- A portfolio value report lists the name of the holding, the number of shares held, the current price per share, the 'cost basis' (ideally the original price plus dealing costs) if you provided one, the percentage gain or loss if there is a cost basis, and the current market value of the holding. You can choose any date in the past for this report, as long as the relevant data is available to *Quicken*. Many investors find it a helpful practice to print value reports monthly and store them in a ring binder.

- An investment performance report shows the percentage return on each of your holdings, taking into account both dividends and capital gain or loss. You can group and subtotal your shares by Type or by Goal. This way of looking at investments, with dividends and capital gains considered as a pair of horses pulling together, is probably more common in America than in Britain. It can throw a very useful light on investment performance, although *Quicken* really needs at least a year's data before this report becomes meaningful.

- An investment income report summarises your investment income and outgoings. Like the performance report, it includes unrealised capital gains as well as gains on actual sales of shares, dividends, and other categories of cash income.

- An investment transactions report lists all the transactions in your account for a specified period: sales, purchases, dividends, and other events such as scrip issues. You can include unrealised capital gains if you like, by pressing `[F8]` as you are setting up the report, even though strictly speaking they are not transactions.

A word of warning: *Quicken* has no capacity to index your capital gains according to the movements of the Retail Price Index. British investors are allowed indexation relief on capital gains, and are also allowed to make gains up to an annual limit without being subject to capital gains tax at all. Thus, as a small investor you may never need to pay this tax.

American investors must pay tax on all capital gains, however illusory they have been rendered by inflation; and they do not enjoy any annual relief. *Quicken* thus can give American users a figure for capital gains which can be a basis for an entry on tax returns. But it does not do the same for British investors, and it does not give any hint of how much of the upward movement (as we hope) of your share prices is due to inflation and how much to the underlying growth of the company.

Share Performance Graphs

Quicken offers three types of graph as tools for portfolio analysis. From the Main Menu, choose View Graphs. From the View Graphs window, choose Investment. For more about the different types of graph, see Chapter Four.

The *Quicken* graphs, as you will see, are not the sophisticated analytic tools beloved of those who study the movements of share prices as ancient Roman priests studied the livers of sacrificial victims. They are none the less powerful instruments to help you assess your progress and plan your future.

● Portfolio Composition is a pie chart. What it tells you is very much determined by the choice you make at the preliminary window. You can choose to have the chart drawn by Security, by Account, by Type or by Goal. Whichever you choose, this type of chart can alert you to situations where your investments are getting out of balance.

● Security will show you how your portfolio is made up, company by company. Experts advise that no slice of this pie should be much more than about 10% of the whole.

● Account will compose the pie of slices each representing one of your Shares Investment Accounts. If you have set things up so that each account contains data about only one share, this pie chart will be identical to the Security one.

● Type may be an even more interesting pie than *Quicken* intended, as you will have substituted Sectors for Types and can now see how your portfolio is distributed among them. Again, watch out for imbalance. No slice of this pie should be more than a quarter of the whole.

● If you specify goals when you define securities, you will be able to see what proportion of your portfolio is devoted to each one.

● Portfolio Value Trend is a stacked bar graph in which each bar stands for a calendar month, the total height of the bar represents the value of your portfolio, and the different-coloured sections are the different securities, accounts, types (= sectors) or goals, depending on which you choose at the preliminary window. This one is invaluable for identifying at a glance the sections of your portfolio which are pulling their weight and the ones that aren't.

● Price History is the graph most people think of first in the context of the stockmarket. It is a line graph or, more likely and more useful, a series of line graphs. Up to 14 different shares or indices can be plotted on the same screen. The more data *Quicken* has the more interesting this one becomes. Each share or index leaves the left-hand side of the screen at its own original price, like horses from a starting gate. The successful ones then go up and the others down, crossing each other as they proceed.

Special Situations

Dividends: When you receive a financial report from a company in which you own shares, it will include a notice about the forthcoming dividend. Somewhere in the report you should find a line something like: 'A dividend of 7p per share will be paid on May 23, 1994, to shareholders whose names are on the Register on March 30, 1994.'

If you are sure you are not going to sell the share before the March 30 date (the date when it goes 'ex dividend', in the language of the stockmarket), you can make the entry in your Shares Investment account right away. Multiply the dividend you find in the financial report by the number of shares you own, remembering that the dividend is expressed in pence so a decimal point will be needed. The answer will be the amount of money you will receive. You will also receive some Tax Credit: for that, see below.

Make the entry (probably with DivX in the Action field) in the Transaction Register of the Shares Investment account, dating it to the date when the financial report says the dividend will be paid. Entering the dividend in advance will help you monitor your cash flow. And if the dividend should go astray, the entry in your *Quicken* records will alert you to the need to hunt it down.

The Billminder (see Chapter Five) works in Shares Investment Accounts. If you put 'Reminder' in the action field of a transaction, you can then use one or both lines of the Security field for the text of a reminder which will appear on the screen of your computer when you turn it on, before you load *Quicken*. This can be used to remind you of investment events such as the due date of an installment payment on a privatisation share or the decision date for a rights issue. Put the date when your decision must be made, and/or your cheque must be in the post, in the date field. To tell *Quicken* how many days in advance you want your reminders to begin, choose Set Preferences from the Main Menu and then choose Automatic Reminder Settings from the Set Preferences menu.

When the need for the reminder is past, find it in the Shares Investment account and put an asterisk (*) or an X in the C field. Or delete the whole entry.

Privatisations: Americans don't buy shares by installments and *Quicken* is not really geared to it. And indeed in the cold, hard world of the 1990s there may be no more such government giveaways in Britain. But there is a way to do it in *Quicken*:

When you are allotted your shares, enter them in a Shares Investment Account with BuyX or Buy in the Action field, just as if the first installment were the entire price. There will be no fees or additional charges in this case.

When you pay the later installments, you need to enter two transactions. First of all, enter XIn to transfer the amount of the installment into the Shares Investment account as cash. Then enter a RtrnCap transaction for an equal but negative amount – this is one of the rare occasions when you will have to type in the minus sign to tell *Quicken* that the amount is negative. Put the name of the privatisation share in the Security field of the RtrnCap transaction. The negative RtrnCap transaction offsets the apparent leap in the stockmarket price of a privatisation share when an installment is paid and provides *Quicken* with an accurate cost basis for the share.

Many privatisations have offered free bonus shares as an incentive to shareholders not to sell their holding. If you ever get any, enter them in *Quicken* with ScrIssue (for scrip issue) in the Action field.

Rights Issues

Sometimes companies raise additional capital by offering shareholders an opportunity to buy new shares at less than the market price. American companies do not use this device, and *Quicken*'s provisions fall somewhat short here too.

If you are offered rights and decide to take them up, enter the purchase in the usual way. The difficulty is that *Quicken* will enter the price of the rights into the price history of the share – where it does **not** belong. As an example, in March, 1993, Bowater offered its shareholders the right to buy new shares at 400p each, payable in installments. The share price at the time was about 480p, and when the rights issue was announced the price rose to over 500p. Shareholders who took up the offer paid a first installment of 132p per share – but '132' did not figure in the 1993 price history of Bowater.

So after you have entered the purchase of your new shares, you will have to go to the Price History window and alter the price. From the investment register, press `[Ctrl]-[U]` for the Update Prices and Market Value screen. Move the highlight to the name of the security whose rights issue you have just taken up. Press `[Ctrl]-[H]`. You will see the Price History window for that share. Move the highlight to the 'wrong' price which has been inserted in the list. Either delete it with `[Ctrl]-[D]`, or press `[Ctrl]-[E]` to edit it to the correct price.

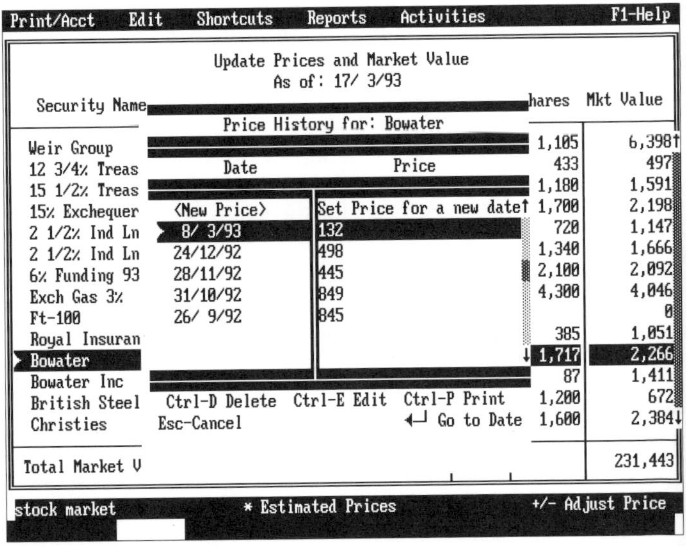

```
Print/Acct   Edit   Shortcuts   Reports   Activities                F1-Help

                     Update Prices and Market Value
                            As of: 17/ 3/93
 Security Name                                          hares  Mkt Value
                     Price History for: Bowater
 Weir Group                                             1,105     6,398↑
 12 3/4% Treas        Date                Price           433       497
 15 1/2% Treas                                          1,180     1,591
 15% Exchequer     <New Price>     Set Price for a new date↑ 1,700  2,198
 2 1/2% Ind Ln     8/ 3/93         132                    720     1,147
 2 1/2% Ind Ln     24/12/92        498                  1,340     1,666
 6% Funding 93     28/11/92        445                  2,100     2,092
 Exch Gas 3%       31/10/92        849                  4,300     4,046
 Ft-100            26/ 9/92        845                                0
 Royal Insuran                                            385     1,051
 Bowater                                              ↓ 1,717     2,266
 Bowater Inc                                               87     1,411
 British Steel   Ctrl-D Delete  Ctrl-E Edit  Ctrl-P Print  1,200    672
 Christies       Esc-Cancel              ←┘ Go to Date     1,600  2,384↓

 Total Market V                                                  231,443

stock market          * Estimated Prices              +/- Adjust Price
```

Fig. 7.8 'Share Price History' window

But it is also possible that you may not want to take up your rights. You can sell them through your stockbroker, and in a case like that of Bowater, they can be quite valuable. Enter the profits in the investment account, with CapGainX in the Action field. That way the money received will be taken properly into account when you prepare an investment performance report. If you sell some of your rights and take up the rest, it is best to enter two transactions: a CapGainX for the sale and a BuyX for the purchase.

Shares in lieu of dividends: An accelerating number of British companies offer shareholders the opportunity to take new shares instead of the regular cash dividend. There are no dealer's charges to pay, and many investors find this a convenient way to add to their holdings. *Quicken* handles this situation well. Enter the new shares in the investment register with ReinvDiv in the Action field.

Since a decision to take shares in lieu of dividends is made freshly every time a dividend is announced, you could decide for cash next time. And you want to know your total dividend income, both cash dividends and dividends taken as shares, in order to estimate future cash flow. With a cash flow report on the screen, do a 'Quick Zoom' by positioning the highlight over one of the figures for Dividends in one of the columns of Actual expenditure and pressing `[Ctrl]-[Z]`. You will see that both reinvested dividends and cash dividends are there.

CHAPTER

Quicken: your financial adviser

FEATURING

- A strategy for saving and investments
- Doing your tax with Quicken

There's no magic button you can press, In *Quicken* or anywhere else, to tell you how to run your finances.

A Strategy for Saving and Investments

Success begins with cash flow. When you are setting up a budget, the figures for Budget Inflows and Budget Outflows at the bottom of the screen keep you on the straight and narrow. Be sure that the difference figure is positive for most months.

From time to time, at least once a month, call up a Monthly Budget report and have a hard look at the bottom line. You can pretty well guarantee that your actual cash flow position will be worse than the budgeted one, at least in your early months of account keeping. That may not matter too much. But is the bottom line positive or negative? That does matter. Your first task is to get it into the black. Maybe not every month, but almost every quarter and certainly every year. Take advantage of *Quicken*'s willingness to summarise your figures by quarter, half-year and year to look at your situation from all angles

Go back up through the categories. You will probably find that overspending is concentrated in relatively few. Some may be the sort (Leisure, Personal, Large Unplanned) which can be adjusted with willpower. Others may require more drastic changes in your way of life.

Once you are living within your means, it is possible to think further. Possible, but perhaps not essential. If you are paying a mortgage, you are making a mighty monthly contribution to your own Net Worth. You are probably also contributing to a pension scheme, and carrying some insurance. There will be whole decades in most people's lives when those three categories will occupy all the spare finance available.

You might find it both interesting and useful to print out and keep a Net Worth report once a year – not more often, or trends will be obscured by the bulk of paper. This is one report that doesn't need to wait until you have been keeping accounts for a while. As soon as you have set up your bank accounts, assets and investment accounts, *Quicken* can produce a valid Net Worth report.

When you reach the stage in life when you have some spare cash to save and invest, you will find so many factors to be weighed that you may be tempted to give up before you start. You will want to try to balance security with steady gain. Complete security is impossible: companies go bust, even the biggest; inflation erodes building society and deposit accounts; houses can go down in value. And steady gain can never be guaranteed.

There are two fairly reliable maxims, although they don't take you very far:

- Don't put all your eggs in one basket; try for a balance between money on deposit, fixed-interest investments, unit and investment trusts, and (riskiest but ultimately most profitable of all) ordinary shares.

- There's no such thing as a free lunch. To put it another way, if an offer seems too good to be true, there's probably a catch somewhere.

In the very long term, nothing beats a well-balanced portfolio of ordinary shares. But before you embark on one, be sure you have enough reserves of cash for the predictable emergencies and some to spare. If you are saving for probable events such as the down-payment on a house, school fees, a daughter's wedding, keep part of the savings on deposit. You may, when the event looms, decide to sell a share that is showing a nice profit. But you don't want to have to sell shares, in case the market is down when you need the money.

Investors who could take a long view sailed through the stockmarket crash of 1987. They took huge losses on paper, like everyone else. But they could afford to wait until things got better. And meanwhile many found that dividend income went up substantially, as companies increased payouts to boost confidence in the 18 months following the crash.

Use *Quicken*'s investment reports regularly. Watch the pie

chart, whether it is showing you individual shares or sectors, to be sure that no one slice is getting too big. The stacked bars will show you which companies or which sectors are gradually increasing in value relative to the whole portfolio, and which others are standing still or sliding backwards. Include at least one index like the FT-SE-100 when you look at line graphs. That way, you will be comparing the performance of your shares with an objective standard. Print out the investment performance report once a year to monitor your over-all results.

Most of all, as the ancient Greeks recommended, know yourself. If you're inclined to panic, resolve to keep calm and give your shares a chance. Dealing costs can eat heavily into profits if you constantly 'churn' your portfolio. If, on the other hand, you're inclined to let things slide in the hope they'll get better one day, resolve to keep a close eye on your portfolio and to take profits sometimes, or at least to cut your losses. It is a good idea to have a hard think about the future of any share in your portfolio which has sunk 10 or 15% below its highest level.

Doing Your Tax with *Quicken*

If your only dealings with the Inland Revenue consist of a gloomy look at the line on your payslip which reveals how much of your hard-earned money never reaches your pocket, you may want to skip this section. But these days more and more of us have to make an income tax return. That includes many married women who have recently started filing returns for the first time because they are now taxed separately from their husbands. Some of them with low incomes have a mighty incentive to fill out a return form – a chance to claim back the tax which has already been deducted from bank and building society accounts and credited on dividends.

Probably the most important thing you can do to help yourself through this annual chore is to resolve to keep everything together. Have a file called Tax: an actual, physical file in the real world, nothing to do with your computer. Have a place where you always keep it. And put everything relating to your taxes in that file upon receipt.

Marking Taxable Categories

The first thing to do is to mark some expense and income categories as 'tax-related'. If you didn't do it when you were setting up the categories in the first place, you can easily go back. From the Transaction Register of any bank account, press `[Ctrl]-[C]` for the Category list. Move the highlight to the Category you are interested in. Press `[Ctrl]-[E]` to edit it. You will see that one of the fields is 'Tax-related'. Put 'Y' for 'Yes'.

And which categories **are** tax-related? Most income categories will be. Some savings schemes are tax-exempt: interest on a Tax Exempt Special Savings Account (a TESSA), for instance. Child Benefit is exempt now (1993) but that could change. It is a good idea to consider your income categories annually when the Chancellor of the Exchequer presents the Budget, just to see if you need to make any changes in the tax-related status of any of them.

Be guided in the last resort by the income tax form itself and the guidelines your tax inspector will have sent with it. Some expense categories may also be tax-related, depending on your circumstances. Perhaps you have some freelance earnings and will be able to deduct expenses from them before you pay tax.

Your Tax Return

The tax return form and its accompanying leaflet of instructions have changed out of all recognition in recent years in the direction of becoming easier to understand. In addition, the Inland Revenue publish a series of leaflets on common tax problems. One example among many: Leaflet IR 87 covers the subject of Rooms to Let. You will find the tax office listed as Inland Revenue in your telephone book, and you can approach them for help even if your actual return is filed with some distant office. Try to help yourself before leaping to the conclusion that you need to pay a professional tax adviser.

Your employer will provide you at the end of the tax year with a P60 form. It shows all the income tax, National Insurance contributions, pension contributions and other deductions which have been made from your pay during the year. You don't need to enter those deductions in *Quicken*.

You may have other income which you have received without any tax deducted from it – freelance earnings, interest on some National Savings products, rent paid to you for property you own. Tax will have to be paid on such income, and it should be entered in *Quicken* under categories which are designated as tax-related. Taxable income which has been paid to you gross (that is, without deduction of tax) should be kept in separate categories from other income which has been received net of tax. Don't lump together the interest from your National Savings Investment Account (paid gross) and the interest from your building society (paid net). *Quicken* has already provided the subcategories 'Gross' and 'Net' under the income category 'Int Inc'. Use them.

If you make any payments by covenant, be sure to enter them in their own category. *Quicken* provides an expense category called Covenants, designated as Tax-Related. If you make a number of payments by covenant, you may even want to use subcategories here to distinguish:

- covenants to charities to assist in their work;

- membership fees in worthy organisations such as the National Trust.

Incidentally, Quicken has marked the category Charity as Tax - Related, because it is so in America. Change that: charitable contributions are not tax - deductible in Britain, except for payments made under Deed of Covenant.

If you have major categories of income from which you deduct expenses, see Chapter Nine on the business uses of *Quicken*. But relatively minor sources of income such as small freelance earnings can be handled very effectively by assigning expenses as they occur to the income category itself.

For instance, when you receive a telephone bill you could split the transaction, assigning part of the total to

'Utilities:telephone' and part to 'Consultancy', according to how much use your records show you have made of the telephone for consultancy purposes during that quarter. Because you are entering a payment, *Quicken* will understand that this is not an addition to your consultancy earnings but a subtraction from them. When you print a *Quicken* Tax Summary report, you will see your consultancy earnings and the corresponding expenses listed together, with the expenses subtracted from the earnings.

When you are ready to fill out your return form, print out a *Quicken* Tax Summary report. You will find on it every transaction in every category you have designated as tax-related. You may want to filter the report to exclude your salary, as you will use your P60 for that entry on the income tax return. You don't need to ask *Quicken* to waste good paper by printing out all 12 or 52 pay days.

For the most part, you will use your accumulated documents and your *Quicken* tax summary together to fill out your tax return. Your bank or building society will provide you with an annual statement showing you the information wanted on the tax form in relation to deposit accounts: the gross amount of income you received from money on deposit, the amount of tax which was deducted, and the net amount of income. You are unlikely to have so many deposit accounts and building society accounts that listing them all on the form will be a burden.

Income received gross must be listed in separate sections of the form. If it is income from which you are allowed to subtract expenses, and if you have entered the expenses in the income category itself as suggested above, filter your *Quicken* Tax Summary report down to that income category only and print out the tax summary report to attach to your tax form.

If you have any dividend income from unit trusts, investment trusts, or ordinary shares, you will have received with your dividend a voucher showing an amount of Tax Credit which you have received as well. From your point of view, the effect is much the same as the tax deduction which was made from the interest you received on your building society account or bank deposit account. But the tax inspector regards Tax Credits differently, and wants from you a list of dividends and Tax Credits received – a list which *Quicken* won't provide.

Tax Credits: a Quicken Workaround

If the program is to settle down and take out British nationality, this is probably the first feature we can expect from *Quicken 6.1.* Meanwhile, we've got to work our way around the difficulty. If you don't have any dividend income, you will probably not be inclined to sympathise much with those who complain about how burdensome it is to make out such a list. But if you do, you will know that it is an unwelcome annual chore and you will be surprised and irritated to find that *Quicken* is not going to offer to help.

What follows is what is known in computer circles as a kludge. Here's what to do:

First, create two income categories: Dividend and Tax Credit, and an expense category called something like Phantom Income.

Next, set up a fictitious bank account with a name like Tax Records.

Now, when you receive a dividend (or shares in lieu of a dividend) enter it your Shares Investment Account in the usual way. Then go to your Tax Records account and enter the dividend again.

● In the Description field, put a full description of the holding which paid the dividend, and the date. Something like '440 British Telecom 2/3/93'.

● In the Deposit field, put the amount of the dividend you have just received, whether you took it as cash or as shares.

● Press `[Ctrl]-[S]` to split the transaction.

● On the first line of the Split Transaction window, put Dividend as the category name. *Quicken* has already filled in the amount.

● On the second line, put Tax Credit as the category name

and fill in the amount of the Tax Credit in the Amount field. The voucher that came with your dividend shows the amount of Tax Credit.

● *Quicken* will automatically add a third line with a negative amount equal to the Tax Credit, in order to make the total for the transaction come out right. Assign it to your Phantom Income expense category.

```
Print/Acct   Edit   Shortcuts   Reports   Activities                F1-Help

DATE  |CHQ NO| DESCRIPTION · MEMO · CATEGORY | PAYMENT |C| DEPOSIT | BALANCE
28/ 2 |      |440 British Telecom 28/2/92    |         | |  12 54  |  99 54
 1992 |SPLIT |                               |         | |         |
----- |  Cat:|dividends                      |         | |         |
15/11 |      |                               |         | |         |

                          Split Transaction
           Category                    Memo                  Amount
  1:dividends                                                 12.54
  2:Tax credit                                                 4.18
  3:phantom income                                            -4.18
  4:
  5:
  6:

                 Enter categories, descriptions, and amounts
 Esc-Cancel      Ctrl-D Delete    F9-Recalc Transaction Total    Ctrl↵ Done

phantom          (Alt+letter accesses menu)
                                                Ending Balance:  £99.54
```

Fig. 8.1 Allocating Phantom Income

● If necessary, put an entry in the Memo field to distinguish joint holdings from those in a husband's or wife's individual name; and also, if you are likely to claim tax back, one to distinguish notional dividends (when you actually took shares-in-lieu) from actual dividends. The Tax Credits on shares- in-lieu count as tax paid in all other respects, but cannot be claimed back. There is thus a possible total of six different memos: His Dividends, Her Dividends, Their Dividends, His Shares - in-Lieu, Her Shares-in-Lieu, Their Shares-in-Lieu. With a bit of luck you won't need all of them.

When you need a dividend list for your income tax return,

select your Tax Records account and create a Summary Report.

- Set the date range for the complete tax year in question, for instance 6/4/92 – 5/4/93.

- Specify 'Description' for the row headings (down the left side).

- Specify 'Category' for column headings (across the top).

- Press [F9] to filter the report. In the Filter Transactions window put Y for Select Categories to Include. If you need different dividend reports to separate out joint holdings from individual holdings and/or shares-in-lieu from cash, put one of your Memo entries on the Memo line in this window. You will next see the Categories list. Ensure that only Dividend and Tax Credit are marked Include.

- Finally, look at the bottom line of the Create Summary Report window: 'Use Current/All/Selected Accounts'. It should be set to C.

File/Print Edit Layout Reports Activities F1-Help

SUMMARY REPORT BY CATEGORY

1/ 1/91 Through 31/ 3/93

JEANMILE-phantom
21/ 3/93

Description	INC/EXP INCOME dividends	INC/EXP INCOME Tax credit	INC/EXP INCOME TOTAL
1083 Weir Group 15/11/91	16.79	5.60	22.39
1200 British Steel 14/1/92	18.00	6.00	24.00
1200 British Steel 19/8/91	34.50	11.50	46.00
440 British Telecom 11/9/91	17.71	5.91	23.62
440 British Telecom 28/2/92	12.54	4.18	16.72
OVERALL TOTAL	99.54	33.19	132.73

phantom (Filtered)
Esc-Leave report

Fig. 8.2 Tax Credit Report

That was a lot of hard work when *Quicken* ought to have done it all for you automatically, but at least the resulting report is pretty close to what you want. Memorise the report to make things easier next year. Press `[Ctrl]-[M]` while your report is on the screen, and give it a name, if you haven't already. You should also 'spend' all the dividends which pile up in your Tax Records account, in order to keep your Net Worth right. 'Spend' them on Phantom Income.

If you like, you can move this report into your word processor to tidy up the headings. See Chapter Ten, *Nuts and Bolts*, for the procedure.

Remember when you are creating other reports to filter out the categories Dividend, Tax Credit, and Phantom Income. Otherwise you will flatter yourself with twice as much dividend income as you actually have. *Quicken* has already recorded your dividend income in its own category, _DivInc. And always be sure you have 'spent' all the dividends in your Tax Records account on Phantom Income before you ask for a Net Worth report.

Quicken cannot help with another of the nightmares of the seriously rich, Capital Gains Tax. American rules for calculating this tax are different from those which apply in this country. The authors of the program, probably wisely, have not tried to incorporate the much more complicated British system. See Chapter Seven on Shares Investment accounts for more on this subject.

CHAPTER

Business uses of Quicken

FEATURING

- Introduction
- Business categories and classes
- Memorised transactions
- Uses of asset and liability accounts
- VAT tracking including depreciation
- Printing cheques
- Paying your staff

Business Uses: an Introduction

Who might benefit?

- People with part-time, freelance earnings who need to keep careful track of expenses and earnings in order not to pay too much tax;

- The self-employed;

- Those on whom Value-Added Tax has imposed the need to learn things about bookkeeping which they'd rather not know, such as
- Contract workers who as registered companies sell their labour to various employers (an arrangement common among computer professionals, among others);

- Corner shops and small businesses which used to operate by throwing all the bits of paper into a shoebox and delivering it to an accountant every so often.

Double-entry bookkeeping is not an easy art to master, even to those used to handling large amounts of money and keeping careful records. Computer programs which automate the journals and ledgers of the traditional double-entry process can be difficult to learn and to use. Accounting programs suitable to larger businesses will seem heavy and rule-bound to a small tradesman or independent professional person.

Quicken is not such a program. Its authors classify it, by contrast, as 'finance software'. Unlike the formal double-entry system, it is easy to learn and to use; and it works 'intuitively' – you do things, on the whole, the way that seems easy and natural.

Quicken's business facilities are a good deal more sophisticated than that description might suggest. VAT tracking and reporting is rigorously implemented. Accrual accounting is possible. Asset and liability accounts for Accounts Receivable and Accounts Payable do the work of traditional journals. *Quicken* will draw up the two classic constituents of financial reports: a Balance Sheet and a Profit and Loss statement.

Quicken's flexible system of Classes and sub-Classes means that you can easily track accounts for a particular project or job.

Quicken will make it possible for many small businesses to take charge of their own finances for the first time. But there are gaps. _Quicken_ won't print your invoices, or your letters to the people delightfully termed in accountants' language 'aged debtors'. If you pay your employees directly into their bank accounts or in cash, _Quicken_ will handle the accounting but won't print advice slips for your staff.

And be careful. Domestic accounts, at least to some extent, can be arranged to please the user and to express his or her own quirky perception of money. Business accounts must meet the more rigorous standards of the auditor, the Inland Revenue, and the VAT Inspector. *Quicken* lacks some of the safeguards of a traditional system: for instance, you can change an entry if you make a mistake. You do not have to make an equal and opposite entry to correct it. *Quicken* will not force you to be consistent in your use of names and codes for customers and suppliers, although it will ensure consistency in categories and Classes (your Chart of Accounts).

Quicken's flexibility means that you have a fair amount of latitude, in business accounts as in personal ones, about how you set things up. Traditional accounting packages are more likely to impose their own system on your accounts. All this makes things easier in a way, but involves obvious dangers. Don't even think of using *Quicken* for your business without:

- reading with care the chapters on 'Using *Quicken* in your Business' in the manual which accompanies the program;

- talking things over with your accountant;

- adopting a rigorous back-up system and using it religiously;

- using *Quicken* in parallel with your present accounting system for three months at least, to make sure that the transfer is going smoothly and that *Quicken* is doing everything you need.

This chapter introduces the features of *Quicken* which are specifically designed for business users, in particular VAT tracking and the special uses of asset and liability accounts. It also covers other features, such as printing your own cheques and memorising groups of transactions, which are suitable for all users but likely to appeal more to businesses.

And remember that *Quicken*-for-business is not a separate program. Most of the techniques which have already been discussed in this book will be needed by business users as well.

If your business is part-time and informal, if you don't know what 'accrual accounting' is and you're not registered for VAT: *Quicken* is the ideal package for you. Just skip the parts of this chapter that don't apply to your situation.

Business Categories

You know already whether you need a separate *Quicken* file for your business. Do you run a registered company? Do you keep business accounts separate from the rest of your finances? or are the rewards of your part-time commercial activities kept in the same accounts as the rest of your money?

To set up a new file, from the Main Menu choose Set Preferences; from the Set Preferences window, choose File Activities; and from the File Activities window, choose Select/Set Up File. As you set up a new file, you will be asked whether you want to use *Quicken*'s Home or Business categories, or both. If you choose to include the Business categories, *Quicken* will automatically turn on VAT tracking. You can turn it off again if you don't need it.

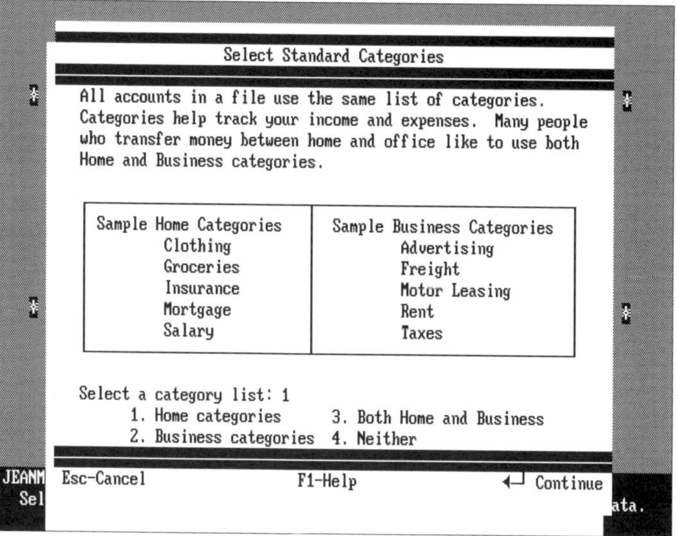
Select Standard Categories

All accounts in a file use the same list of categories. Categories help track your income and expenses. Many people who transfer money between home and office like to use both Home and Business categories.

Sample Home Categories	Sample Business Categories
Clothing	Advertising
Groceries	Freight
Insurance	Motor Leasing
Mortgage	Rent
Salary	Taxes

Select a category list: 1
1. Home categories 3. Both Home and Business
2. Business categories 4. Neither

Fig. 9.1 Selecting the Business Category List

Of course you can change the Business categories, and add to them, just as with the Home ones. See Chapter Two. If you are currently using a traditional bookkeeping system in which you have a Chart of Accounts each designated with a number, you can use those numbers as category names and give the purpose of each account as its Description. If you do that, you will want *Quicken* to print both the number and the description – for instance '4001 Sales' or '4002 Returns' – on your reports. From the Set Preferences menu, choose Cheques and Report Settings. Enter B in the field 'In reports, print category Description/Name/Both.' On the other hand, you may be delighted, if your accountant approves, to get away from account numbers altogether and just use words.

In business accounting, you should assign every transaction to a category. A more formal accounting package would force you to do so. As you know by now, *Quicken* will report as 'Other' any income or expense which is not categorised. In business, that's not a good idea.

If you're running a small business from your personal

account, you should probably assign all business transactions to a Class as well as to a category. If, for instance, you own a cottage which is available for holiday lettings, you would enter your receipts under some such heading as 'Rent/Dunroaming' and your expenditure as 'Cleaning / Dunroaming', 'Advertising / Dunroaming' and 'Repairs / Dunroaming'. In this way you would be able to call up a report of all the transactions relating to your business even though the money itself is entangled with the stuff of everyday life.

Perhaps you're a dentist, a joiner or a computer consultant: that is, perhaps your business is the sort in which you offer services to a client. In that case, you can use Classes to keep separate the income and expenditure relating to a particular project or client. If you designate separate projects by number, you can use those numbers as Class names, just as you may have used account numbers from your Chart of Accounts as category names.

A decorator, for example, might have expense transactions such as 'Wallpaper/Lysias Road' or 'Paint/job 204'. A purchase of supplies to be used on more than one job can be split between Classes in the familiar way.

A property developer converting houses into flats might need a whole range of categories and subcategories:

Professional fees
Architect
Estate Agent
Planning department

Contractors
Builder
Plumber

Supplies
Building Materials
Fittings
Kitchen Equipment

Classes could be used to relate each transaction to the conversion of a particular property.

Subclasses can also be used, and do not, like subcategories, need to be defined in advance. The developer could keep the expenses separate for different flats in the house he was working on, by defining them as 'Fittings /Rowfant Road/Flat 1' or 'Kitchen Equipment / Rowfant Road/Flat 3'. *Quicken* in fact imposes a limit of 15 characters (letters and spaces) as the total for the Class or Classes of any one entry, so you would have to resort to abbreviations: 'Kitchen Equipment / Rowfant/ Flat2' would do nicely.

Quicken's categories, subcategories, sub-subcategories, Classes and subclasses means that there are almost endless possibilities for sorting and arranging transactions and preparing reports.

Traditional bookkeeping with *Quicken*

If you aren't registered for VAT and have never heard of a ledger, you can probably skip this section.

In traditional bookkeeping parlance, it is easy to see *Quicken*'s use as a cash book, in which you record both sales and purchases at the time that money changes hands. But even businesses which would prefer it otherwise do a great deal of trading on credit these days. An accounts system without a sales ledger, a purchase ledger and a means of predicting cash flow would not be a great deal of use.

Some of what follows is going to make fairly heavy reading. *Quicken*, here as elsewhere, leaves the choice to you of how to set things up. In the end, you're only going to do it one way, and that way will seem easy and natural when you're doing it. But you're about to read about the choices, and there's a danger of getting bogged down in them.

Try this:

- Read this section with your computer on and *Quicken* loaded;

- Set up a new file, as described above; choose Business

Categories for it; call it something like Test; set up a current account with a balance of some sort, an Asset account called AR for Accounts Receivable, and a Liability Account called AP for Accounts Payable.

● And as you read, try it out. Type in a few of your own invoices and watch *Quicken* do the VAT split. Record some of your receipts and outgoings.

That way, you'll see how easy it is as you go along. And you'll decide on the system that's best for your circumstances by actually trying it out.

Accounts Receivable: Open an asset account and call it AR for Accounts Receivable.

When you issue an invoice, enter it in this account as an Increase. Your assets have increased because you are owed more money. If you are registered for VAT and are accounting in the normal way, your liability for VAT arises at this point. See the section on VAT accounting later in this chapter – *Quicken* makes it easy.

Put the invoice number in the Ref field (or in the Memo field if it is more than six digits long). In the Description field, put the name of the your customer, and his or her code number if you have been using such a system and want to carry on with codes.

In the Category field, classify the income – `[Ctrl]-[C]` will call up a list of your categories corresponding to the Chart of Accounts of your old system. Remember that you can go on using the code numbers from your Chart of Accounts as the category names if you like. Memorise the transaction (see Chapter Five) if you are sending this invoice to a customer you are likely to deal with again. That technique will help you be consistent in entering transactions.

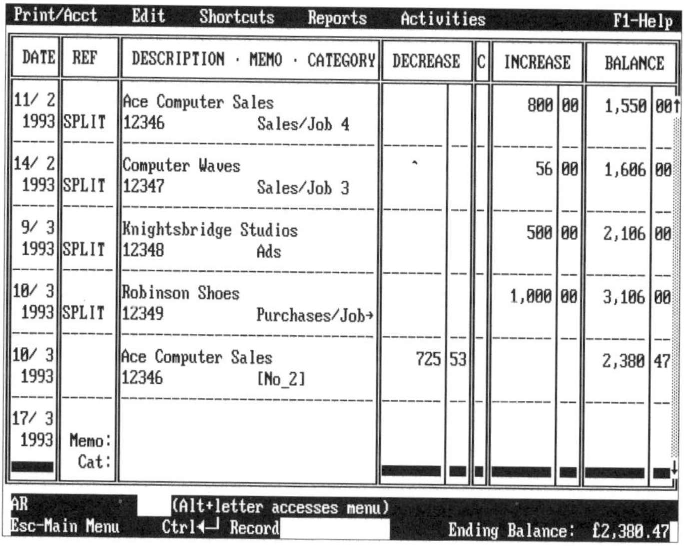

Print/Acct Edit Shortcuts Reports Activities F1-Help

DATE	REF	DESCRIPTION · MEMO · CATEGORY	DECREASE	C	INCREASE	BALANCE
11/ 2 1993	SPLIT	Ace Computer Sales 12346 Sales/Job 4			800 00	1,550 00
14/ 2 1993	SPLIT	Computer Waves 12347 Sales/Job 3			56 00	1,606 00
9/ 3 1993	SPLIT	Knightsbridge Studios 12348 Ads			500 00	2,106 00
10/ 3 1993	SPLIT	Robinson Shoes 12349 Purchases/Job→			1,000 00	3,106 00
10/ 3 1993		Ace Computer Sales 12346 [No_2]	725 53			2,380 47
17/ 3 1993	Memo: Cat:					

AR (Alt+letter accesses menu)
Esc-Main Menu Ctrl↵ Record Ending Balance: £2,380.47

Fig. 9.2 Accounts Receivable

You can add a Class to the category if you want to pigeon-hole the income by project, perhaps, or salesperson. When you are dealing with major customers, you might want to use the customer name as a Class. Some freelance workers with their own registered companies will work for one employer for considerable stretches of time, submitting invoices for work done. If you are in that position, you may want to set up an entire asset account devoted to your current employer. *Quicken*'s flexibility makes it easy to work out a system to suit your particular case, but it can also present you with an embarrassment of choices. That is why it is so important to bring your accountant in at the planning stage.

When you receive payment, make another entry in the AR asset account. This time, decrease the asset: you're not owed as much as you were. Put the money in the Transaction Register of the account where it actually goes by recording a *Quicken* transfer from the asset account. There are several ways you can do this, and the choice will depend very much on the way your business works:

● You can go back to the original invoice, split the transaction, enter the payment as a negative amount and transfer it to the account where you are going to put it, and mark the invoice as paid with an asterisk (*) in the C for Cleared column. It is important to mark invoices as paid so that they do not turn up in Accounts Receivable reports.

● Or you could enter the payment in your Accounts Receivable asset account as a separate transaction, with the amount of the payment in the Decrease column. Enter the customer name and the invoice number as you did on the original invoice. Put the name of the account receiving the money in the Category field, to indicate a transfer of funds. Mark the transaction as Cleared with an asterisk in the C column. Find the original invoice and mark that as Cleared as well.

● If you have customers who pay something on account, covering several invoices or less than one, use the customer name as a Class when entering the invoices in the first place. When you receive payment, make a separate entry in Accounts Receivable. Type the customer name and the invoice number or numbers exactly as you did when entering the original invoices. In the category field, put the name of the account where the money is going, with the customer name again as a Class. That way, you can quickly get a report of how much that customer owes you.

Under this system you have not marked the separate invoices as Cleared, so an ordinary Accounts Receivable report would give a misleading impression. Remember to memorise the payment transaction if there are several details which are likely to reappear.

Accounts Payable: You can handle Accounts Payable with a liability account, corresponding to the Accounts Receivable asset account. But you may not need to.

● You can reverse the procedure just described for Accounts Receivable. Set up a liability account. Call it AP for Accounts Payable. Enter in it the invoices you receive as they arrive, in the Increase column because a bill you must pay increases the amount you owe. Assign the payment to a category, splitting the transaction if you like and using Classes as well as categories to define the payment with all required precision. Then tell *Quicken* to memorise the details of the transaction so that you can use it again.

When you pay an account, enter the transaction in the register for your current account. Transfer the amount to your AP account by putting 'AP' in the category field. Then go to the AP account and mark the invoice you have just paid and the payment itself with an asterisk in the Cleared column. That is necessary to keep your Accounts Payable reports accurate. You will have to set up the report yourself: see Accrual-Basis Accounts Payable in the section of this chapter on business reports.

● You could do without a liability account and use *Quicken*'s cheque-writing facility. You don't actually have to print *Quicken* cheques in order to make use of this feature. See the section below on cheque-writing. The 'A/P by Vendor' report, described in the reports section of this chapter, is based on the cheques you have 'written' in *Quicken* to pay each of your accounts.

● If your main interest in Accounts Payable is to forecast your cash flow, you could enter future payments directly in your usual transaction register, dating them to the date on which you expect to make the payment. See Cash Flow Forecasting in the section on business reports later in this chapter. You can set up Standing Orders to appear in your transaction register up to 99 days in advance, postdated to the date on which they will actually be paid. Be sure to take advantage of that option if you decide on this system.

Depreciation: You can use an asset account to track depreciation of capital equipment. The self-employed are often allowed to claim depreciation expenses against their earnings. The procedure is described below, in the section on VAT, but you don't need to use *Quicken*'s VAT-tracking if VAT doesn't apply to you.

VAT

If you're registered for VAT, you'll need a separate *Quicken* file for your business accounts. After you have set it up, choose Set Preferences from the Main Menu. Choose

Transaction Settings from the Set Preferences menu. Be sure that the last line in the Transaction Settings window, 'Activate VAT-tracking features', is set to Y for Yes.

If *Quicken* hasn't automatically presented the table of VAT rates as you were setting things up, choose 'VAT Table' from the Activities menu on the toolbar. And whenever VAT rates change, go back to the VAT Table and record the changes there. There is room for 10 different rates, but you are unlikely ever to need more than the first three on the list: 'E' for Exempt, 'N' for Zero-rated and 'S' for Standard. Fill in the current rates for all three. Type in a rate of 17.5% as '17.5', not '.175'.

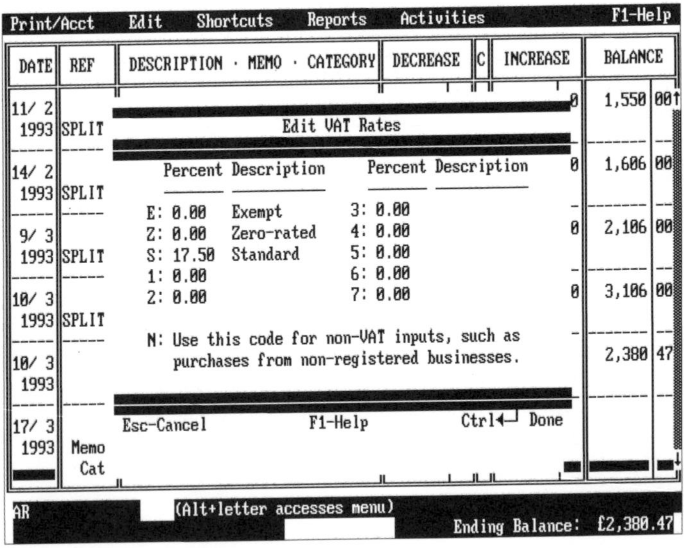

Fig. 9.3 'VAT Rates' window

You need to assign VAT codes to each of the income and expense categories in your list. If you loaded *Quicken*'s list of business categories, codes have already been assigned. Call up the category list in the usual way by pressing `[Ctrl]-[C]` from any transaction register. You will see the VAT code, 'E' or 'S', listed with each category name. Check down the list to make sure that all the codes are right.

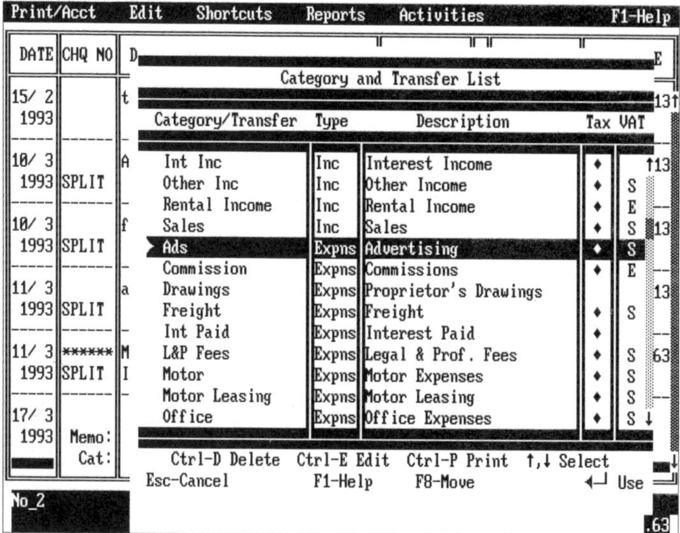

Fig. 9.4 Assigning VAT Codes to Categories

You can also turn VAT-tracking off for a particular account if you need to. Select that account from the list of accounts and press `[Ctrl]-[E]` to Edit the details.

Quicken has automatically set up a VAT Control Account for your business. You will find it listed with your other accounts, and you can examine it at any time. If you have more than one business separately registered for VAT, you must keep the accounts in separate *Quicken* files. If the structure of your businesses is very similar, you may be able to save time by copying one file and using that as the basis for another: see Chapter Ten, *Nuts and Bolts*.

Accrual accounting: The normal VAT tax point is the day you issue or receive an invoice, not the day you get or part with your money. To keep VAT accounts properly, you will have to set up an asset account for Accounts Receivable and a liability account for Accounts Payable, as already described. Be sure that VAT-tracking is turned on for the asset and liability accounts. Turn VAT-tracking off for your current account.

When you issue or receive an invoice, enter the gross amount in the register of your AR or AP account. Enter the category, and a Class if you like. When you press **[Enter]** after typing in the category, the Split Transaction/VAT Entry window will open automatically. You will see that the gross amount you typed in has been separated into a Net Amount and a VAT Amount. Press **[Ctrl]-[Enter]** to confirm. And that's all there is to it.

When you later receive or pay out the money, enter the transaction in your current account. Remember, VAT-tracking should be turned off for this account. Transfer the gross amount to the AR or AP account.

Cash Accounting: If you have the approval of your VAT office, you can use cash accounting for your VAT returns. In cash accounting, the liability for VAT arises when money changes hands, not when invoices are issued. Do not set up AR and AP accounts. Turn VAT-tracking on for your current account. From there on, the procedure is exactly the same: when you have entered all the details of the transaction including the category, the VAT Entry window will open automatically, showing your transaction divided into a Net Amount and a VAT Amount. If you choose a category coded E, for Exempt, the window opens anyway but the entire amount of the transaction appears as a Net Amount.

Cash and Accrual Accounting: Perhaps you have the approval of your VAT office to use cash accounting but still need to keep track of the invoices you have sent out.

Set up an asset account for Accounts Receivable. Turn VAT-tracking off for this account. When you issue an invoice, enter the net amount only in Accounts Receivable.

Turn on VAT-tracking for your current account. On the category list, find your AR account. Move the highlight there and press **[Ctrl]-[E]** to Edit. You will see the Edit Usual VAT Code window. Put 'S' for Standard. That does not mean that VAT-tracking is turned on for your AR account. It means that transfers to that account will be treated like payments to any other expense or income category coded 'S'.

When you receive payment, enter the gross amount in

your current account. Put 'AR' in the category field to transfer the money to Accounts Receivable. You will see the VAT Entry window with the amount split into Net Amount and VAT Amount as usual. Press `[Ctrl]-[Enter]` to confirm.

Now when you look at your AR account, you will see that the net amount only has been transferred to it, as a decrease in the amount of the asset.

Depreciation

To track depreciation of capital assets, set up an asset account called something like Equipment. If you are registered for VAT, you will need to assign a VAT code to this account. When you have set the account up, locate it on the category list. Press `[Ctrl]-[E]` to Edit. In the Edit Usual VAT Code window, put 'S' for Standard. That means that transfers of money to your Equipment account will be assessed for VAT.

When you buy a capital asset such as a computer or a fax machine, enter the purchase in your current account with the name of the asset in the Description field and the name of the asset account, Equipment, in the category field to indicate a transfer to that account. The VAT window will open as usual. Press `[Ctrl]-[Enter]` to confirm *Quicken*'s division of the amount into Net Amount and VAT Amount.

Now look in your Equipment account. You will see that, quite properly, only the Net Amount has been transferred here. *Quicken* will not calculate depreciation automatically, but you can make a regular entry (in the Decrease column) of the amount agreed with your tax inspector by which you are allowed to depreciate your assets. Assign the amount to an expense category called Depreciation.

Don't forget the *Quicken* calculator. Start typing the depreciation entry, and position the cursor in the Decrease column. Press `[Ctrl]-[O]` for the calculator. Type in '25%' (or whatever rate of depreciation you are allowed), `[*]` (meaning 'times'), the current agreed value of the asset, and finally `[=]`. There's your answer: this year's depreciation figure. `[F9]` pastes it into the register.

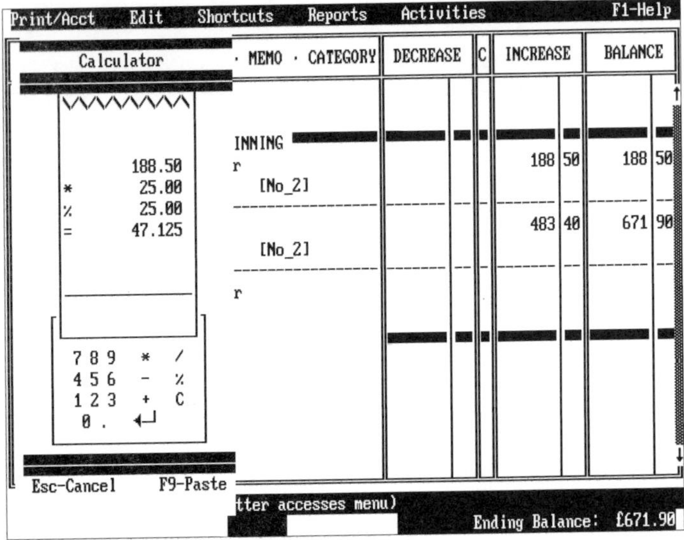

Fig. 9.5 Calculating Depreciation

Since you have an expense category called Depreciation, your Profit and Loss report will now automatically include it. For a specific report on Depreciation only, see the section on business reports later in this chapter.

Fixed Assets: If you want *Quicken* to prepare a Balance Sheet for your business, you will need to set up asset accounts to include all your assets. Talk to your accountant about this one.

VAT code 'N': You may have dealings with a supplier who is not VAT-registered. The code for such transactions should be 'N', not 'E' (although the result in both cases is no VAT to pay), and the transactions should be included on your VAT return.

If you are going to deal with such a supplier regularly, you should devise a separate expense category and give it the VAT code 'N'. For a one-off transaction, open the category list, find the expense category you want to use, and press `[Ctrl]-[E]` to Edit it. Change the VAT code to 'N' and then enter your transaction. Open the category list again and change the code for that expense category back to 'S' immediately.

Letting *Quicken* Write your Cheques

The cheques themselves must be ordered from Intuit, the software house *Quicken* comes from. Various styles are available, and Intuit will print your company logo on them. A brochure and order form are included with the *Quicken* package. The company guarantees, among other things, that the cheques will work with your printer and be acceptable to your bank.

The procedure is quite simple. From the opening menu, choose Write Cheques. The Write Cheques screen is laid out like a real cheque. All you have to do is fill it in. If you are 'writing' the cheque in *Quicken* the day the bill arrives, date the cheque for the day you actually intend to send it off. *Quicken* can use these postdated cheques for an Accounts Payable report, as you will see in the section in this chapter on business reports.

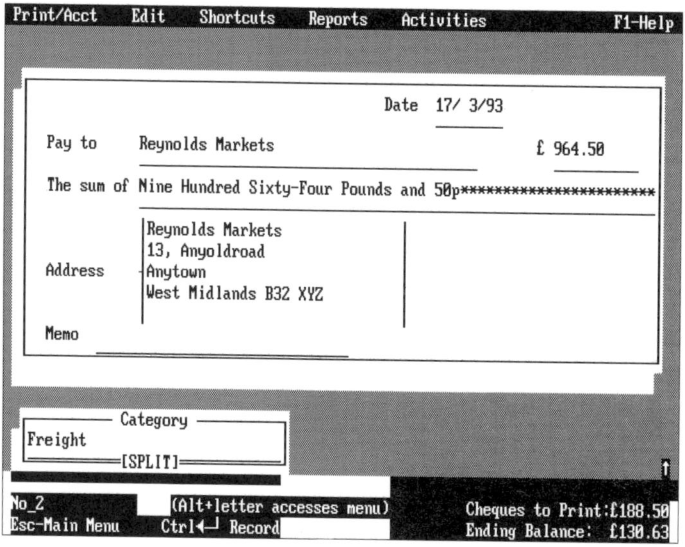

```
Print/Acct   Edit   Shortcuts   Reports   Activities                F1-Help

                                          Date  17/ 3/93

 Pay to     Reynolds Markets                                 £ 964.50

 The sum of Nine Hundred Sixty-Four Pounds and 50p************************

            Reynolds Markets
            13, Anyoldroad
 Address    Anytown
            West Midlands B32 XYZ

 Memo

 ---------- Category ----------
 Freight
 ===========[SPLIT]============

No_2              (Alt+letter accesses menu)       Cheques to Print:£188.50
Esc-Main Menu     Ctrl←┘ Record                    Ending Balance:  £130.63
```

Fig. 9.6 A Quicken Cheque

If you want to use the window envelopes which Intuit also provides, you can type in the address of the payee on the cheque. You should assign the transaction to a category –

Quicken will make the entry in the Transaction Register without any further help from you. And if the account on which you are writing the cheque has VAT-tracking turned on, *Quicken* will automatically split the amount of the cheque into Net and VAT.

If you write frequent cheques to the same payee, you can get *Quicken* to memorise the details. On the computer-screen cheque form, type in all the information which will be repeated for future payments. Include the payee's name and address if you are going to use window envelopes. Then press `[Ctrl]-[M]`. *Quicken* will highlight the information you have just typed in and ask you to confirm that you want it to be memorised.

To use the memorised cheque in the future, press `[Ctrl]-[T]` at the Write Cheques screen. You will see a list of your memorised transactions. Choose the one you want.

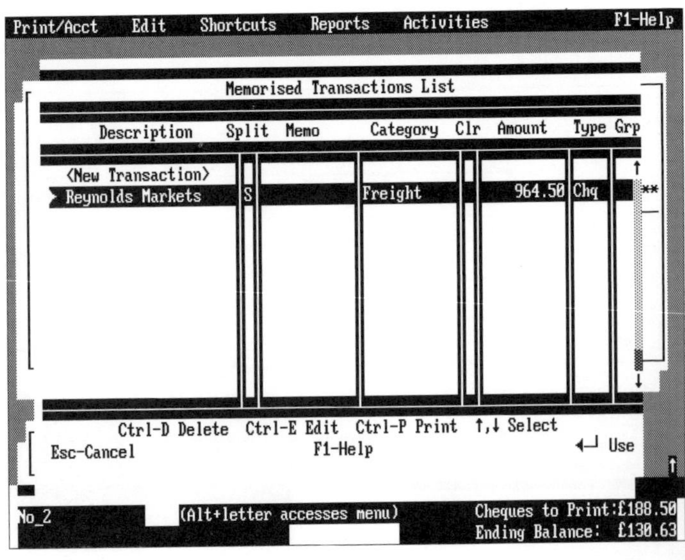

Fig. 9.7 Memorised Transaction List

Some people use this cheque-writing facility to provide reminders for themselves about when payments are due, or to furnish a basis for an Accounts Payable report. *Quicken*'s arm- twisting reminder system is called the Billminder: read about it in Chapter Five. You can still write the actual cheques by hand when the time comes. If you do that, you will have to go to your transaction register and fill in the cheque number and the date of payment yourself.

Actually to print the cheques you have written, or some of them, choose Print Cheques from the Print/Acct menu on the toolbar. The Print Cheques screen allows you to specify a date. The program will then print all cheques up to that date, but not beyond. It also allows you to select which cheques to print. If you choose that option, you will see a list of the cheques you have written. You can select them individually.

If you have 'written' your cheques well in advance, you will want to tell *Quicken* to date them correctly when they are actually printed. From the Main Menu, choose Set Preferences. From Set Preferences choose, Cheques and Report Settings. Set 'Change date of cheques to date when printed' to 'Y'.

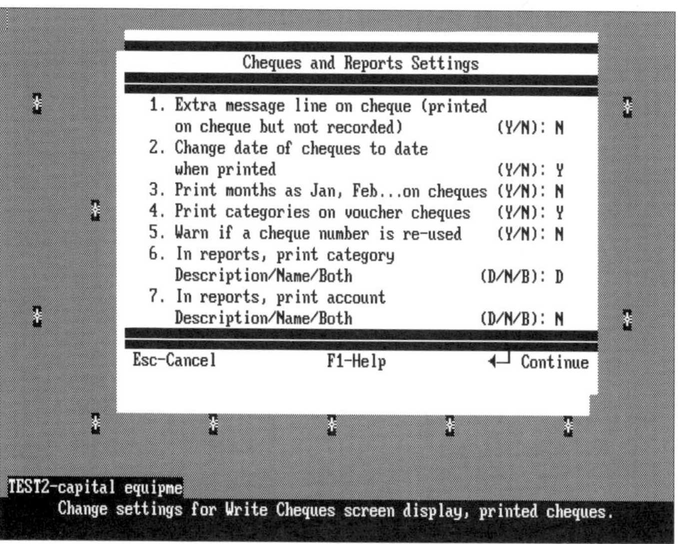

Fig. 9.8 Cheques and Reports Settings

When *Quicken* has written a cheque for you, the cheque

number in your transaction register is automatically filled in. When you originally 'wrote' the cheque, the number appeared as a row of asterisks.

If you have ever used a computer printer, you will know that there are a truly extraordinary variety of things which can go wrong when you try to print out the words and figures you see on your computer screen. The Intuit manual covers a wide range of possible mishaps and their remedies in its clear and well-illustrated chapter on cheque-writing. If all else fails, the company promises to sort out your troubles by telephone. If it can't, it guarantees to refund the money you paid for the printed cheques.

Paying Your Staff

Even if your 'staff' is an army of one, you will be glad to have *Quicken*'s help with the accounting chores. The procedure that follows sounds complicated. To some extent, it is. But you have probably paid staff before, and will know about the inevitable deductions. And when you have once got things set up in *Quicken*, it will never be complicated again.

First, you must set up Payroll expense categories and Payroll liability accounts. The liability accounts are for the amounts you deduct from your employees' wages and pay on their behalf. That becomes money you owe to the Inland Revenue or the pension fund: therefore a liability, a special form of Accounts Payable. The expense categories are, as usual, there to classify the expenses you bear: the wages themselves, and the additional employer's contributions you must pay. The name of each expense category must begin with the word 'Payroll' if the Payroll Report mentioned in the next section of this chapter is to work.

Under the Payroll expense category, set up subcategories, not for deductions but for for the various payments you make to each employee and on his or her behalf: gross pay, employer's National Insurance, employer's pension contributions. For each expense which is not part of the employee's gross pay, begin the subcategory name with the letters 'Comp' for 'Company'.

Next, set up the liability accounts: one for each type of deduction you make from your employees' pay, such as National Insurance and Pay-As-You-Earn income tax; and one for each payroll-related expense of your own, such as employer's pension contributions. Use names for these liability accounts which begin with the word 'Payroll', such as 'Payroll-NI' and 'Payroll-PAYE'. Be sure that the names of the liability accounts are different, however slightly, from the names of the expense categories.

When the expense categories and the liability accounts have been defined, you are ready for your first payday. The procedure is essentially the same whether you make the payment directly from your bank account into your employees' accounts, write cheques by hand, pay in cash, or write cheques in *Quicken*.

Set up Standing Orders if you pay directly into your employees' bank accounts: you can make adjustments to the actual sums at the time of payment if you need to. See Chapter Two for the procedure. Type in your employee's name and the net amount of pay which he or she will actually receive. Then press `[Ctrl]-[S]` to split the transaction.

On the first line of the Split Transaction window, put 'Payroll:Gross'. *Quicken* will have filled in the Amount column with the net amount. Move the cursor there and type in the gross amount instead. *Quicken* will immediately enter a negative amount on the next line in the Amount column. It should be equal to the total amount of all the deductions.

```
Print/Acct   Edit   Shortcuts   Reports   Activities                F1-Help

DATE  CHQ NO  DESCRIPTION · MEMO · CATEGORY   PAYMENT  C   DEPOSIT   BALANCE
18/ 3         John Smith                       482 63
1993   Memo:
        Cat:
                           Split Transaction
             Category                    Memo                    Amount
  1:Payroll:gross                                                 600.00
  2:                                                             -117.37
  3:
  4:
  5:
  6:
                  Enter categories, descriptions, and amounts
 Esc-Cancel       Ctrl-D Delete    F9-Recalc Transaction Total   Ctrl←┘ Done

My bank account    (Alt+letter accesses menu)
                                               Ending Balance:  £543.00
```

Fig. 9.9 A Payroll Transaction

The lines of the Split Transaction window are numbered for you. On the following lines, starting with 2, enter under Category the various Payroll liability accounts (Payroll-NI, Payroll-PAYE, Payroll-Pension and any others). Enter the amounts of the deductions in the Amount column as negative amounts. When you have entered them all, there should be no extra amount, positive or negative, on the following line. If there is, go back and check your arithmetic.

Move down to line 9 if VAT-tracking is turned on for the account from which the payment will be made, or line 17 if VAT-tracking is turned off.

You must now make some double-entries for payroll expenses which are not part of the employee's gross pay. Start with 'Payroll:Comp NI', one of your expense categories, and enter as a positive amount the National Insurance contribution which you as an employer must make for this employee. On the next line, put 'Payroll-NI', the liability account, and enter the same sum as a negative number. Repeat this process with any other costs which you bear as an employer.

And that's it. Awful the first time, but henceforth *Quicken* will make the entry in all the appropriate accounts automatically. All you have to do is double-check the accuracy of the pay and deductions.

If you write a cheque by hand, you might want to use the Standing Order method anyway. Just replace *Quicken*'s entry of StdOrd in the Chq No column of the Transaction Register with your actual cheque number when the time comes.

Or you could make the entry directly in the Transaction Register and memorise it. Start with the date and the employee's name. Type in the net amount, the actual money the employee will receive. Then press `[Ctrl]-[S]` to open the Split Transaction window, and proceed according to the instructions for Standing Orders above. Then memorise the transaction: see Chapter Five. In the future, you need only go to the Memorised Transactions list and choose your employee's name.

If you pay by cash, the choices are the same as paying by cheque, only of course you will use the Transaction Register of your cash account.

If you pay with *Quicken* cheques, start writing the cheque by putting the date and the employee's name. Now press `[Ctrl]-[S]`, before you put any amount, to open the Split Transaction window.

The procedure from here is similar to setting up a Standing Order. On the first line put 'Payroll:Gross'. Fill in the gross amount of pay as a positive number. On the following lines, enter the Payroll liability accounts (Payroll-NI, Payroll-PAYE, Payroll-Pension and any others). Enter the amounts of the deductions in the Amount column as negative amounts. Move down to line 9 if VAT-tracking is turned on for the account on which you are writing the cheque; or line 17 if VAT-tracking is turned off.

Now make the double-entries for payroll expenses as above: 'Payroll:Comp NI', the expense category, for the employer's (ie, your) National Insurance contribution as a positive amount; 'Payroll-NI', the liability account, for the same amount as a negative number. Repeat this process with any other costs which you bear as an employer.

Finally, press [F9] to calculate the total cheque amount. *Quicken* will subtract the deductions from the gross pay and take you back to the cheque screen. Finish filling it out, and then press [Ctrl]-[M] to memorise it.

For all methods except Standing Orders: If you have more than one employee, memorise the whole payroll as a group – for memorising groups, see Chapter Five.

When you write a cheque (to the Inland Revenue or a pension fund or whatever) to pay for items deducted from employees' gross pay and for employer's contributions, enter the cheque as a transaction in your current account and put in the category field the name of the relevant liability account – Payroll-NI, Payroll-PAYE or any other. *Quicken* will enter a decrease in the liability account. If you write one cheque to the Inland Revenue for both PAYE and National Insurance, you can split the transaction between the two liability accounts.

Business Reports

There are lots of reports available, and you can set up others to your own requirements. See Chapter Four for a more detailed discussed of the procedures. From the Main Menu, choose Create Reports. From the next window, choose Business Reports.

Profit and Loss Statement: This is in fact the Summary Report described in Chapter Four.

Cash Flow Report: Again, identical to the personal cash flow report.

A/P by Vendor: This report is generated from your unprinted cheques. Enter each invoice you receive by 'writing' a *Quicken* cheque to pay it. Date the cheque to the day you receive the invoice. Then when you choose this report, *Quicken* will give you a list of your suppliers with the total owed to each. There will be a column for each month in the period covered by the report, and a column for the overall total. Remember that if this report is to be useful you will have to 'write cheques' for all of your Accounts Payable, even the ones paid by Standing Order or credit card.

Remember that if you are using *Quicken* to print your cheques, the dates on your cheques will have to be changed to the actual date of printing. See the section on 'Letting *Quicken* write your cheques' earlier in this chapter to see how to tell *Quicken* to do that automatically.

VAT-tracking was done when you wrote the cheque in the first place, so this system is not suitable for those who pay VAT in the normal way, on an accrual basis. If you are in that position you will need to keep the date of the invoice – the VAT tax-point – separate from the date of the actual payment. See 'Accrual-basis Accounts Payable' further on.

A/R by Customer: If you are using an asset account for Accounts Receivable, this report will give you a summary by customer of how much you are owed, with a separate column for each month covered in the report. If you are going to use this report, it is essential that you mark the invoices in your AR asset account as Paid, with an asterisk in the C column, when you receive your money. The report summarises all the invoices which are not marked Paid.

Job/Project: If you have been assigning income and expenses to separate jobs or projects or clients by using *Quicken*'s Classes, this useful report will give you your totals. Each row of the report is an income or expense category, listed down the left-hand side of the page. Each column is a separate job or project, headed by one of your Class names. A final column on the right gives an overall total.

Payroll: If you are using *Quicken* to handle your payroll, and if you have set things up as described in the previous section, this report will summarise all your payroll income and expenses by category with a column for each employee. *Quicken* does this by looking for the categories and transfers which begin with the word 'Payroll'. All your various payroll expenses were set up as subcategories under Payroll, so they will appear correctly here.

Balance Sheet: This resembles the personal Net Worth report. It combines the balances in all the accounts in your file to show your assets and your liabilities. It also incorporates the equation fundamental to bookkeeping: Assets equal Liabilities plus Capital. So on this report, the difference between assets and liabilities is shown as 'Equity' (another term for Capital) rather than 'Net Worth'.

Domestic users can leave bits out and still enjoy getting a rough general idea of their net worth. Businesses need to be sure that their assets are correctly listed in asset accounts before a Balance Sheet has any significance. You will certainly need your accountant's advice about valuing assets.

Missing Cheque: Identical to the personal Missing Cheque report.

VAT Detail: For this one, you will usually supply a date range covering the current VAT quarter. The report lists all your VAT-related business transactions, first the Outputs and then the Inputs. It is subtotalled by month, although you can choose any other interval, or none at all. Most usefully there will be a separate list at the end of the report of transactions without VAT codes. That should help you spot any mistakes.

Vat Summary: Again, you will probably specify the current accounting period as the date range for this report. It will give you all the information you need to fill out your VAT 100 form.

Those are the pre-set reports listed on the Business Reports menu. But there are others you might want to work out for yourself. Remember that it is easy to memorise a report.

Single Job: If you have been using Classes to separate your accounts for different jobs or projects, you may want a report on one project only. Create a summary report. Subtotal by month, and choose Month for the column headings. Filter the report, putting the Class name for the job or project you are currently interested in on the line saying 'Class contains'. See Chapter Four for greater detail.

on the techniques of creating custom reports and filtering them.

Cash Flow Forecasting: Personal users forecast cash flow by looking at the bottom lines of their budget screens. Predicting cash flow accurately is, if anything, even more important to business users. One way to handle it is to set up an asset account called Forecast Receipts in which you enter all other expected income besides the invoices you have already put in Accounts Receivable. You might be expecting bank interest, for example, or rent on a property your company owns. Enter expected payments directly in your transaction register, using the date on which you intend to make the payment.

You can then call up two different cashflow forecasts;

- Cash Receipts and Disbursements: Set up a Transaction report. Exclude any accounts which track non-cash expenses such as Depreciation. Set the date range from tomorrow forward. Subtotal by week.

- Sources and Uses of Cash: Create a summary report totalled by category or a transaction report subtotalled by category. Alternatively you could have the totals by payee. Set the report organisation to 'Cash flow basis' by choosing Other Options from the Layout menu on the toolbar when the report is displayed.

And you can use your Forecast Receipts asset account in an Accounts Receivable report. Set up a Transaction report. Set the date range from tomorrow. Subtotal by week. Choose 'Selected accounts' on the Create Transaction Report window. Select Forecast Receipts and Accounts Receivable.

Account Balances: Choose this option from the first menu you see after you choose Create Reports from the Main Menu. Set the report to monthly intervals. This report provides valuable insight into past cash flow.

Accrual-Basis Accounts Payable: If you pay VAT on the normal basis, the tax-point is the day you receive an invoice. In that case you will certainly want to set up a liability account for Accounts Payable. The other methods, 'cheque-writing' in *Quicken* or entering postdated payments directly in your transaction register, will not be good enough because they do not clearly distinguish the date of the invoice from the date of payment.

To get an Accounts Payable report in that situation, choose Create Reports from the Main Menu and then choose Summary Report from the next menu. Set a date range to include all your unpaid bills. Choose Payee (your suppliers) for the row headings and Month for the column headings. Include only your Accounts Payable liability account in this report.

Some additional reports you might want, based on your Accounts Receivable asset account:

- Receivables by Customer. If you used Classes to distinguish different customers when you entered your invoices, you can create a summary report with Class for the row headings and Month for the column headings.

- Customer Payment History. For this one, you will need to record the date of payment in the Memo field of an invoice when you go back to mark it as paid. Create a transaction report subtotalled by payee. The Date column on the left of the report will show the date of your invoice. The Memo column will show the date you received payment.

- Depreciation: if you have set up an Equipment asset account to track depreciation, you can create a summary report limited to the Equipment account only. Specify Category for row headings and Month (or Quarter or Year) for column headings.

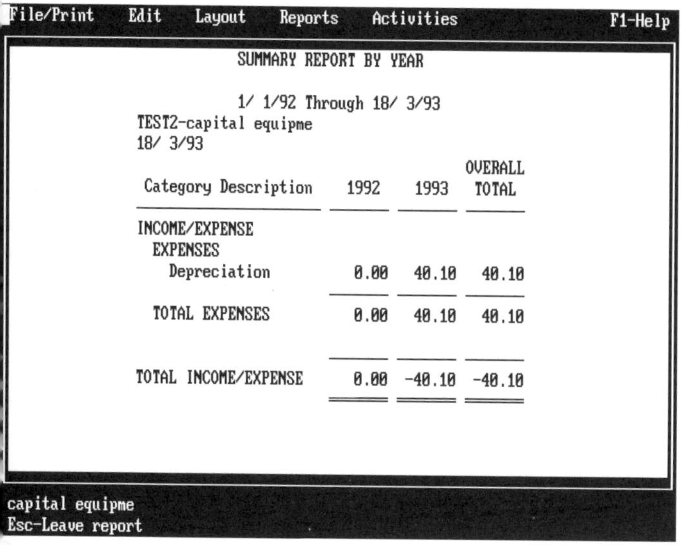

```
File/Print   Edit   Layout   Reports   Activities                F1-Help

                  SUMMARY REPORT BY YEAR

                  1/ 1/92 Through 18/ 3/93
         TEST2-capital equipme
         18/ 3/93
                                                      OVERALL
          Category Description      1992     1993     TOTAL
         ------------------------  -------  -------  -------
         INCOME/EXPENSE
           EXPENSES
             Depreciation            0.00    40.10    40.10
                                   -------  -------  -------
           TOTAL EXPENSES            0.00    40.10    40.10

                                   -------  -------  -------
         TOTAL INCOME/EXPENSE        0.00   -40.10   -40.10
                                   =======  =======  =======

capital equipme
Esc-Leave report
```

Fig. 9.10 Depreciation Report

CHAPTER

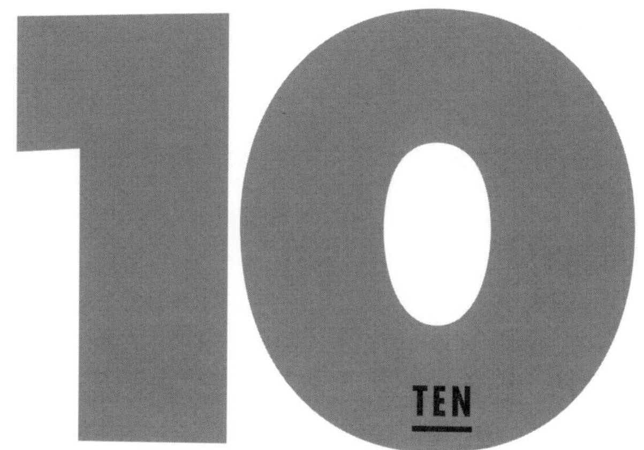

Nuts and bolts

FEATURING

- Backups
- Passwords and read only files
- Changing preferences
- Copying a file
- Importing and exporting data

This chapter contains a rag-bag of techniques you might need some day or other: how to protect your *Quicken* data with a password so that no one but you can see it; how to make an archived *Quicken* file 'read-only'; how to copy a *Quicken* file; how to import and export data; how to change the way *Quicken* looks.

Backups

And one technique that you need today: making backup copies of your data. Modern computers are very reliable, but it remains true that death, taxes, and hard disk failure are three of a kind.

You do not need to worry about power failure or accidentally turning your computer off. *Quicken* saves your work to the computer's internal hard disk as you go along. Every transaction is saved as soon as you hear that cheerful beep when you confirm an entry or an alteration with `[Ctrl]-[Enter]`.

The level of security you choose will depend on how important your data is to you. As a domestic user, you could, if you had to, revert to the dark ages when you didn't bother to keep accounts. You'd hate it, but you could still pay your bills and fill out your income tax return. As a business user, the loss of your 'books' could, at the worst, mean ruin.

One comfort: the routine of security will seem tedious in Week One but will become second nature. Soon, switching off without making backups will be as unthinkable as going to bed without brushing your teeth: and no harder.

You can if you like take responsibility for your own fate. When you want to make a backup, choose Set Preferences from the Main Menu; choose File Activities from the next menu; choose Back Up File from the next one. *Quicken* will then walk you through the process.

But you might as well let *Quicken* remind you. From the File Activities menu, choose Back Up Frequency. You will see that you can set the frequency to 'Never', 'Always', 'Weekly' or 'Monthly'. Go on: choose 'Always'.

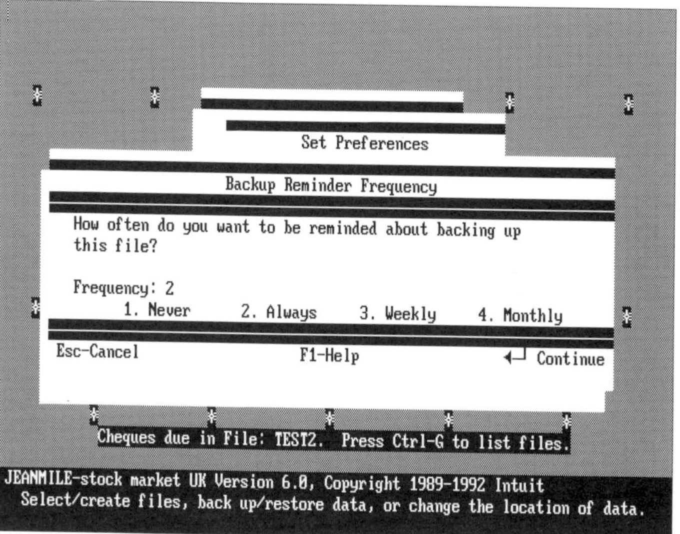

Fig. 10.1 'Backups Reminder' window

If you do this, *Quicken* will present you with a reminder screen whenever you choose 'Exit' from the Main Menu. You will be helped through the backup process. If you have just been having a look at your data and haven't changed anything, *Quicken* will know and will skip the reminder. And if you can't be bothered with backups today, just press **[Esc]** when you see the reminder screen. What about the backups themselves? For a domestic user, this routine should be adequate:

- Provide yourself with two new, formatted floppy disks, 'floppy' in name only if your computer uses the newer 3.5-inch disk format. Label them '*Quicken* backup' and '*Quicken* weekly backup' (or '*Quicken* monthly backup' if you use the program less frequently). Have a third new formatted disk available.

- Keep the first disk, '*Quicken* backup', near your computer, so that you can reach it without standing up. Use it to back up every *Quicken* session.

- Once a week, if you're a daily user, make your backup on

the second disk instead. If you use the program less frequently, use the second backup disk near the first of every month.

● Eventually you may find that one disk is not enough to hold your backup files. *Quicken* will prompt you to insert a second disk when it is needed. That's why you started off with a third new, formatted disk prepared. When you reach this stage, you might like to think about reducing the size of your *Quicken* files. See the section in Chapter Five on how to close a financial year and archive your data.

A business user should be even more careful. Start with six new, formatted disks. Label three of them '*Quicken* One', '*Quicken* Two' and '*Quicken* Three'. The other disks are for use when your data files extend over more than one disk. Backup alternate *Quicken* sessions on '*Quicken* One' and '*Quicken* Two'. Use '*Quicken* Three' instead once a week. Keep '*Quicken* Three' in a different room from your computer, in case of fire or theft.

Experts say that floppy disks gradually become less reliable with use. You don't want to use your *Quicken* files to put this theory to the test. Once a year, replace the whole set of backup disks. You can always use the old ones to backup less important data from some other program. Can't you?

And when disaster strikes? Install *Quicken* on the hard disk of your new computer, if need be, and choose Restore File from the File Activities menu. *Quicken* will give you all the guidance you need from there.

Protecting your Data

If you feel you need to protect your data from others who have access to your computer, *Quicken* is ready to help. But you should think of more fundamental security first. Can the building in which your computer is housed be made more secure? Should you lock your office more regularly? Many computers today are sold with a physical lock fitted. Can you find your computer keys? Should you be using them? What about keeping your *Quicken* data on a floppy disk you carry with you in pocket or handbag? If your computer uses 3.5-inch disks that's perfectly feasible: they're tough little things.

To do that, from the Main Menu choose Set Preferences; from Set Preferences, choose File Activities. From File Activities, choose Set File Location.

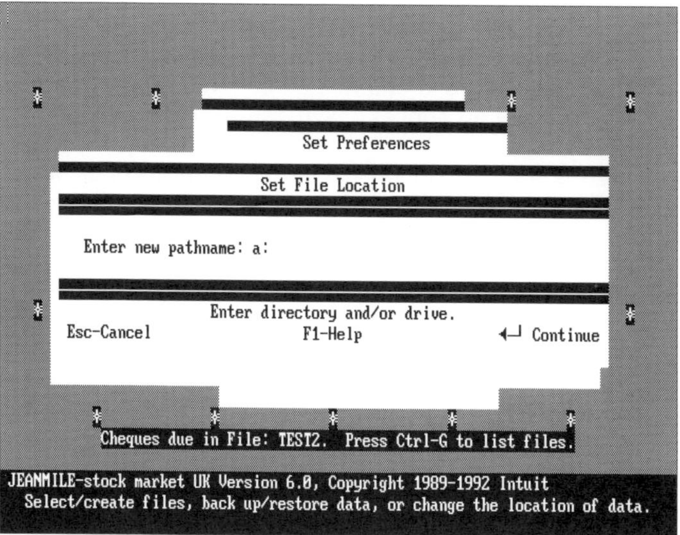

Fig. 10.2 'File Location' window

Specify one of your floppy disk drives, A: or B:, as the new location. If you do this when you first start to use *Quicken*, none of your financial records at all will be on the hard disk of your computer. But the making of backups becomes even more important, of course, because you have added the danger of losing your data disk to all the other hazards computer flesh is heir to.

To protect data by setting a password, choose Set Preferences from the Main Menu; choose Password Settings from the next menu. *Quicken* will ask you to type in the password you want to use. You will have to confirm your choice by typing it a second time.

Once you've done it, you've done it. You can choose

Password Settings again at any time and change the password, or do away with passwords by simply pressing [Enter] at the Change Password window. But you can't get into your file to do that or anything else without first entering your password. If you forget it, you will have to telephone Technical Support at Intuit. That will be embarrassing.

If you have more than one *Quicken* file, perhaps because you have more than one business registered for VAT, or run a share portfolio in a foreign currency, notice that the password you set applies only to the current file.

There is another option under Password Settings which you might want to consider. You can set a transaction password which must be entered before transactions earlier than a specified date can be altered. It is you, of course, who specify the date. You might want to do that when you have effectively closed an accounting period by filing a VAT or income tax return.

You could go a step further, and use a transaction password as a device to make an entire file read-only. If you archive some of your older data in the way described in the section in Chapter Five on 'Ending a Financial Year', set a transaction password on the archive file with a date well in the future. If for any reason you ever do want to change the archive file, well, you know the password. Transactions protected in this way can still be read, printed, and used in reports.

Changing Preferences

Not only is *Quicken* a highly flexible program in the way it allows itself to be used, it is also obligingly willing to let you change the way it looks and behaves.

From the Main Menu, choose Set Preferences. From the Set Preferences menu:

- Screen Settings will let you play around with the way *Quicken* looks. There are settings suitable for monochrome displays (common on portable computers), and, a thoughtful touch, one for colour blind users of colour monitors. The

Menu Access choice on the Screen Settings menu will let you change the way the whole program presents itself: if you prefer, you can use function keys to get to the toolbar (instead of the [Alt] key and the first letter of a word) and numbers (instead of highlighted letters) to make a choice from a menu.

- Transaction Settings lets you turn off *Quicken*'s beep, and decide whether the program should ask for confirmation when you try to do something that could prove rash.

- Cheques and Reports Settings lets you make changes on points of style affecting the way your cheques and your reports are printed.

The other choices, like Printer Settings and Password Settings, are more strictly functional.

It is a good idea to return to Set Preferences after you have been using *Quicken* awhile, and wander around among the choices. It could turn out that a feature which has been driving you crazy can be put right by changing a 'Y' to an 'N' somewhere.

Copying Files

A specialised feature approached through the Set Preferences menu is 'Copy File' on the Files Activities menu. If you are familiar with MS-DOS, the operating system of your computer, you will know about the procedure for copying files. *Quicken* means something slightly different when it says 'Copy File'. Your *Quicken* 'file' consists of four separate DOS files. In addition, *Quicken* has stored information about your accounts and your preferences in other files of its own. When you choose 'Copy File' from the Files Activities menu in *Quicken*, you are embarking on a more complicated procedure than the DOS Copy command. Fortunately, *Quicken* handles the complications.

The procedure for copying files has been discussed in the section on Completing a Financial Year in Chapter Five. *Quicken* invites you to give a name to the new file; to specify the date range to be included; to decide what to do with uncleared transactions prior to the date range you specify, and so forth. If you are copying a complete file, none of the decisions will be at all difficult.

But perhaps you have two similar businesses separately registered for VAT. You want to copy the **structure** of your first file to use, perhaps with modifications, for your second business. But you don't want to copy any of the transactions. Here's what to do:

- From the Write Cheques screen or a transaction register in your first file, press `[Alt]-[P]` to select the Print/Acct menu from the toolbar. Choose Export from that menu.

- You will see the 'Export Transactions to QIF File' window, but don't worry, you're not going to export any transactions.

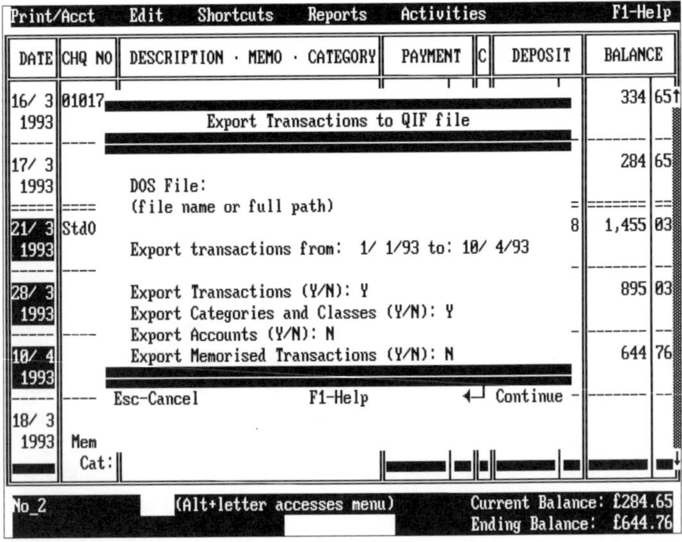

Fig. 10.3 Copying a Quicken File

- You will be asked for a name for the export file. What you are creating here is a 'bridge' file to carry information from your present *Quicken* file to a new one. The name you give to the bridge will be needed only temporarily, like the bridge itself. But choose something you will remember. *Quicken* suggests that all such files be given the extension '.QIF'.

● You can then choose what aspects of the present file to export: transactions, with a date range; categories and classes; accounts; and memorised transactions. You will put 'N' for transactions and 'Y' for categories and classes. Whether or not to copy accounts and memorised transactions depends on your circumstances.

● Set up, if necessary, your new file, with at least one account. From within the account in your new file, choose Import from the Print/Acct menu on the toolbar.

● At the Import window, type the name of the bridge file you just created. Again you will be asked for a decision about whether to import transactions, categories and classes, etc. Answer as you did before.

All this is a great deal easier than it sounds.

Exporting Data

You might want to transfer *Quicken* data to your word processor or a *Lotus 1-2-3*-compatible spreadsheet. It is easily done.

Set up a report containing the data you want. If you are going to move it to a word processor, try to devise a report no wider than your computer screen. If you are moving to a spreadsheet, on the other hand, choose 'Full Column Width' from the Layout menu on the toolbar so that *Quicken* does not truncate anything.

When you are ready, choose Print Report from the File/Print menu on the toolbar. From the Print Report window, choose 4, 'Disk (ASCII file)' for a word processor or 5, 'Disk (*1-2-3* File)' for a spreadsheet. You will be asked to give the file a name before it is exported.

In your word processor, eliminate side margins altogether before importing the ASCII file. Otherwise columns of figures may go askew. Your word processor should have a facility for importing ASCII files.

If your spreadsheet is *Lotus 1-2-3* the *Quicken* file can be imported directly. You will probably have to widen some of the columns in order to view your data. For *Excel*, use the DOS command RENAME to change the extension of the *Quicken* file from .PRN to .CSV. Other spreadsheets which can read *Lotus 1-2-3* files should work as well.

Maintaining Separate Files in *Quicken*

As you know, there are situations when you need to have more than one *Quicken* file: perhaps because you run more than one business, or have a stockmarket account in a foreign currency. Don't create additional files unless you have to, although it is easy enough to do: there are great advantages in having all your accounts in one file if circumstances permit.

From the Main Menu, select Set Preferences. From Set Preferences, choose File Activities. From File Activities, choose Select/Set Up File.

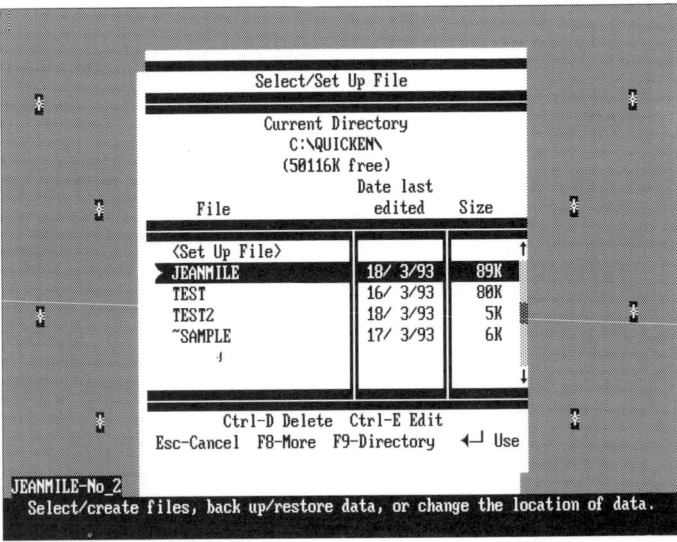

Fig. 10.4 Setting Up Your Files

Return to this screen by the same route whenever you need to switch between files during a *Quicken* session.

And notice that if you have set up *Quicken* to remind you

of anything, you will get the reminder both when you switch your computer on and at the *Quicken* Main Menu at the beginning of a session, even if the reminder applies to a file which is not your current one.

GLOSSARY

An extract from the PC ANSWERS glossary. Courtesy of Ian Sharpe, editor of PC ANSWERS magazine.

086, 8088, 80286, 80386, i486: See CPU.

087, 80287, 80387, i487SX: See maths coprocessor.

ccess time: Used in connection with storage devices such as memory and hard disks. Refers to the average time taken to begin delivering stored information from the point at which it was requested. On a hard disk this would be the time taken to find and open a file, and begin to deliver information to the PC. The lower this time, the higher the speed.

daptor: Normally refers to the circuit, usually in the form of an expansion card, that connects to the monitor to generate the video display.

NSI: American National Standards Institute.

NSI.SYS: One of the many standards defined by ANSI is a system of codes that can be used to control aspects of the screen such as the colours of the text and its background. The codes are contained in the text and instead of being printed on are acted upon by the terminal/screen. A terminal that obeys these commands is known as an ANSI terminal. Ansi.sys is a program supplied with DOS that, once installed, remains in memory. It intercepts text on its way to the screen, looking for and obeying ANSI codes - making the PC emulate an ANSI terminal, in effect.

Once you know how to output ANSI codes to the screen, you can control colours, cursor position and so on. You can also modify the operation of the keyboard.

Apple Macintosh: A desktop computer that doesn't run the same programs as IBM-compatible PCs, and doesn't normally run MS-DOS. Instead it runs an operating system that looks similar to Windows, the latest version of which is called System 7. Macs are used a lot in the world of DTP and graphic design.

Application: A program or collection of programs that makes the PC carry out a specific job such as being a word processor or a database system.

ASCII: American Standard Code for Information Interchange. Usually pronounced 'askey'. Computers only deal with numbers - see byte and bit - so each character of text must be represented by a numeric code. Capital A is 65, B is 66 and so on. ASCII is a widely used list specifying which numbers represent which characters. The list is limited, so under Windows it has been superseded by the more extensive ANSI character set. This uses the same code numbers as ASCII for common characters, so plain text files can be moved between Windows and DOS without becoming unintelligible.

AT: Advanced Technology. An IBM model designation for its first PC with an 80286 CPU. Now often applied to later machines with i386 and i486 CPUs.

Autoexec.bat: A text file full of DOS commands, most of which you would normally have to type in every time you started up the PC. Instead, as soon as DOS has loaded and before it presents you with the command line, it automatically reads the file and executes the commands it finds there, just as if you were typing them in.

Backup: The process of copying data from one storage medium, for instance a hard disk, to another such as floppy disks or a tape streamer. The back-up copy can be used if the original is accidentally destroyed.

BASIC: Beginner's All purpose Symbolic Instruction Code. One of the easiest languages for writing programs. Many PCs come supplied with a version of BASIC.

Batch (.BAT) file: A text file whose name ends in .BAT. It mostly contains instructions that could have been typed at the DOS command line. When you type the name of the batch file (without the .BAT) at the command line, the instructions in it are read and acted upon, just as if you were typing them in. Batch files save you time and effort if you run the same sets of instructions repeatedly.

BBS: Bulletin Board System A computer attached to a modem and running special BBS software. People with modems and comms software can dial the BBS so that the computers are linked via the phone line. You can then leave messages for other users, retrieve (download) files left by other people (shareware programs, interesting pictures and sound files for example) or copy files to it (upload) for other people to download.

BIOS: Usually refers to programs permanently recorded in a chip (a read-only memory, or ROM) fitted to the PC. DOS and applications can use them to perform basic input and output operations like screen printing, hence the name Basic Input/Output System. The in-built BIOS can be (and is) extended by additional software loaded from disk when the PC starts up, which then resides in RAM. Some expansion cards contain BIOS chips so that programs can access the facilities they provide.

Binary: Numbers written in base 2 where a digit can only be 0 or 1. Decimal 1, 2, 3, 4, 5 translate as 1, 10, 11, 100, 101. See byte and bit. At heart, computers deal only with numbers, and they are stored in binary format.

Bit: A byte is divided into eight bits Each bit can represent the digits 1 or 0. Eight digits in binary notation can form numbers whose decimal values are between 0 and 255. In a memory chip, a bit is really a tiny electronic switch.

Boot: The process the PC goes through when it starts up - it checks itself, then loads the operating system from disk. Re-boot means to force the PC to go through its start-up sequence again.

BubbleJet: Canon's proprietary name for its ink jet printers.

Bus: A circuit that carries data between different parts of the computer. See expansion bus and local bus.

Byte: A unit of storage capacity in a computer - a memory cell. It will hold a number between 0 and 255. These numbers can be used as codes to represent text characters (See ASCII) and other data. They can also represent instructions to the CPU.

Cache (disk): An area of memory used to store a copy of data recently read from or written to a hard disk. When a program requests data from the disk, if it is in the cache it can be supplied a lot more quickly than bringing the disk mechanism into play. The result is to speed up operation of the program. A disk cache is usually set up by a special utility.

CD-ROM: Compact disc read-only memory. Like an audio CD but used as a storage medium for programs and data. Very high capacity but the PC cannot normally save information on it, only read from it. Used to distribute a large quantity of material that doesn't need to be changed.

Cell: See spreadsheet.

Centronics: See parallel port.

CGA: Colour Graphics adaptor. IBM's first attempt at a colour display adaptor. Chunky characters and graphics coupled with limited colours make it seem crude by today's standards.

Character: A letter, numeral, punctuation mark or special symbol that can be displayed on the screen or printer.

Clone: A PC not made by IBM but which will run the same software and use the same hardware add-ons as a genuine IBM machine.

CMOS: Complementary metal oxide semiconductor. Used to make chips that need to run with low power requirements. The CMOS RAM in an AT-class machine is a small area of battery-powered memory used to store certain settings while the PC is switched off, such as the type of hard disk fitted and the current time.

Config.sys: A text file containing commands, read by DOS as it loads. It differs from autoexec.bat in two ways: Firstly, it is read earlier in the boot sequence before DOS has fully loaded and deals with more fundamental configuration options. Secondly, the instructions in it would not be recognised by the DOS command line as ones it could deal with.

Comms: Short for communications. The act (or art) of exchanging data between computers, often via the telephone system using a modem.

Compatible: Used in many contexts, such as IBM-compatible, Laserjet-compatible or SoundBlaster-compatible. The IBM PC, Hewlett Packard LaserJet printer, and the SoundBlaster sound card were all products that became so popular they dominated their markets. Much software was therefore written to work with them.

CPU: Central processing unit - the chip with ultimate control of your PC's hardware. It is told what to do by programs. The CPU chips used in PCs were designed by Intel and given an identifying number: 8088, 8086, 80286, 80386 and i486, in increasing order of power and capability.

Crash: A serious program malfunction which has unpredictable results. Often the PC locks up entirely, and you have to re-boot.

DAT: Digital Audio Tape.

Data: Information in a computer system being processed by a program, for example names in a database or figures in a spreadsheet. Confusingly, the data being processed may be another program, for instance in the context of a disk cache 'data' may include program files.

Database: A program that stores information - for example a list of names and addresses or a book catalogue - in such a way that it can easily be retrieved by use of searching and sorting facilities. The information is typically stored in records, each record corresponding to a card in a conventional index.
Within each record are one or more fields. If the database contained a list of names and addresses, for example, each person would have their own record within which their name, the lines of their address, and the telephone number would have their own fields.

Default: When something must be specified, for example when an installation program asks you to name the hard disk directory into which it will copy files from a floppy disk, the default is a setting built into the program which is used if you choose not to specify something of your own.

Device driver: A piece of software that loads into memory when the PC starts up and stays there until it switched off. In this sense it is like a TSR, but it usually loads earlier in the boot-up process by being named in config.sys. A device driver becomes an extension to DOS, and is therefore more tightly integrated with the system than an ordinary TSR. It has the special purpose of enabling other programs (including DOS itself) to make use of devices they wouldn't otherwise know existed or how to control. A mouse driver is a good example. A device driver may alternatively enhance the use of a device the system already knows about. Ansi.sys is one example, disk-doublers like Stacker are another.

Dingbat: See Zapf Dingbats.

DIP: Dual in-line package - a chip where the connectors form two lines, one down each long side. You will also read about DIP switches, which are tiny blocks of switches mounted directly on a circuit board and used to set up particular options. These often appear on printers, motherboards and expansion cards.

Directory: A self-contained area of the disk created and given a name with DOS's MD command (alternatively MKDIR) - MD LETTERS, for example, to create a directory called LETTERS. A directory is an aid to organisation used to keep files related to a particular purpose so that they may easily be found. You can think of them as drawers in a filing cabinet, except that you can have drawers within drawers. For instance in a directory called documents you might have two more directories, one for letters, the other for your novel.

A directory contained within another is known as a subdirectory. The two terms are often used interchangeably. A newly-formatted disk has only one directory. All other directories are created within it by people or programs, or within directories they have created previously. This original top-level directory is known as the root directory. DOS applies commands such as DIR to the currently selected directory - See the CD (alternatively CHDIR) command in your DOS manual.

Disk: General term covering various types of media used to permanently store program and data files. In most cases they can be both read from and written to by the PC. Many types (though not all) rely on a magnetic coating similar to that employed on audio tapes. Before information can be saved on such a disk, it must be recorded with a pattern of concentric rings (tracks) which are subdivided into sectors.

Disk doublers/compressors: Programs (usually in the form of a device driver) that use file compression technology to automatically compress and decompress information going to and from the disk. The disk thereby appears to be larger (nearly twice the size) than it really is.

DOS: Disk operating system. Also See MS-DOS and DR DOS .

Dot matrix: A printer where the characters and graphics are formed from a grid of dots (matrix) produced by wire pins.

Download: See BBS.

DPI: Dots per inch. Used as a measure of resolution.

DR DOS: Digital Research Disk Operating System. A competitor to MS-DOS that will run the same software and obey the same or similar commands.

Drive: In the context of a disk it is the mechanism that holds the storage medium and reads and writes the information.

Driver: A piece of software that enables programs to access particular pieces of hardware and make use of their facilities. An example would be a new printer with facilities unavailable in other models. A driver would be written to allow popular existing programs (Windows, for example) to use the new features.

DTP: Desktop publishing. An application program for designing pages of graphics and text as found in magazines, newsletters, adverts and the like.

EGA: Enhanced graphics adaptor. A step up from CGA offering a sharper image by virtue of putting more dots on the screen, plus more colours.

EISA: Extended industry standard architecture. A non-IBM design of PC more advanced than AT and XT machines. It is a competitor to MCA.

EMS: See expanded memory.

EXE file: Files whose names end in .COM or .EXE are programs. Internally the two types are structured slightly differently. COM files are an older specification and limited to 64K in size. The EXE file structure was developed to overcome this and other limitations.

Expansion Bus: See Bus. The PC has what is known as an open architecture, meaning that companies other than the original designer (IBM) have free access to technical information that enables them to build extra circuit boards (known as expansion boards or expansion cards, or just cards) that can be plugged into sockets (expansion slots) provided for the purpose.

These boards add capabilities not found on the motherboard, for example in many cases the video and disk controller circuits are in the form of expansion cards. In traditional PC design, the expansion slots all sit on a circuit that acts as a communication highway between the CPU and the cards. Visualise the CPU as the city at the end of a motorway, with the expansion slots being junctions. Unlike a motorway, however, communication along the expansion bus is slower than in the core circuitry (the city streets), so any feature provided on a card will operate more slowly than if it had been part of the core design.

Expansion card: A circuit board that fits into an expansion slot.

Expansion slot: A socket inside the PC into which can be plugged circuit boards that add extra capabilities to the machine.

Expanded/extended memory: Different ways of adding memory beyond the basic 640K. Expanded memory (also known as LIM EMS - Lotus Intel Microsoft Expanded Memory Specification after the companies that defined how it should work) can be fitted to all PCs. Hardware restrictions dictate that it works differently to normal memory, and programs have to be specially designed to use it. Expanded memory acts like a notebook which applications can employ for additional data storage capacity, flipping between pages as required.

Design limitations in the 8088 and 8086 CPU chips mean that PCs fitted with them cannot have extended memory - you need an 80286 or better. Extended memory simply adds more RAM on top of the basic 640K which is normally accessible by MS-DOS-based programs. DOS has this limitation owing to design restrictions imposed in the days when 640K was more memory than most people even dreamt of owning.

More recent products such as Windows and OS/2 can take full advantage of extended memory, and by extension so can programs specially written to be run from within those environments. By using a memory manager, extended RAM can also be made to mimic expanded RAM if that is the only type that your software will work with.

FDD: Floppy disk drive.

Field: See database.

File: A self-contained body of information stored on disk that can be retrieved at a later date. It can be a program, a document from a word processor, an address list from a database, a year's sales figures from a spreadsheet or whatever. The file is given a name - the filename - so that you can refer to it.

File compression: It is often possible to reduce the size of a file by re-arranging the data it contains into a more compact format. For instance an area of the file may be identical to another. The duplicate area can be eliminated, and a small marker left in its place. When the file is expanded (de-compressed) back into a usable state, the marker indicates that the eliminated data must be reconstituted by copying the first instance of it. This is just one of many ways data can be compacted.

Some files are automatically compressed/ decompressed by the application that writes and reads them. For example, PCX graphics files incorporate a simple compression technique. Utility programs such as PKzip and LHA also exist which will compress one or more files and combine them into a single storage (or archive) file. The utility will also de-compress the files when they are needed. Also see disk doublers/compressors.

Floppy disk: A flexible disk - although it may be contained in a rigid case - that is removable from the drive. Two sizes are available for the PC: 5.25-inch and 3.5-inch. Each size comes in two or more capacities. Floppies have less storage space, are slower and less reliable than other types of disk.

Font: Strictly speaking, a particular size and style of a typeface, for example 14pt Times Italic. Times is the design (the typeface), Italic is its style (slanted), and 14pt (14 point) is a measure of the height of the characters. In computing the term font is often used to mean typeface.

Format: Used mainly in two contexts. To format a disk means to lay down a structure of tracks and sectors ready to receive programs and data. A file format is a set of rules governing the way information is structured inside a file. Any program that knows the rules can read or write files that conform to them. For example, graphics files are often in a format known as PCX. In theory, a painting, DTP or word processor program that understands the rules governing PCX can make sense of PCX files produced by other software.

Gb: Gigabyte - 1,024Mb, or 1,048,576K.

Graphics: Any screen or hardcopy output where pictures are constructed from tiny dots allowing almost anything to be drawn.

Graphics accelerator: A special type of video card with circuits designed to speed up screen operations involving graphics by taking over a lot of the work normally performed by the CPU. Windows and Windows applications benefit particularly, since screen operations are a significant bottleneck on performance. An accelerator card only improves applications for which special drivers are supplied, probably with the card itself. With other applications it behaves like an ordinary VGA or SVGA card.

GUI: Graphical User Interface. Basically another name for WIMP.

Hard disk: A combined disk and drive mechanism usually permanently fixed inside the PC, but removable and portable external versions exist. Much faster and far higher capacity than a floppy disk, so they are frequently used for primary day-to-day storage.

Hardware: The electronics and mechanical units that make up the computer and its peripherals.

HDD: Hard disk drive.

Hercules: A company which produced a mono display adaptor combining MDA-standard text-only output with a special graphics mode. Hercules produces other products, including top-end colour adaptors, but its name is often used to refer to this old widely-adopted mono standard.

High memory: The first 64K of expanded memory. It is given a special name because, owing to a design quirk in 80286 and later CPU chips, late versions of DOS can make use of it even though in theory it should be inaccessible. Making use of high memory enables DOS to leave more of the basic 640K free for application programs.

HMA: The high memory area. Some people use this to mean upper memory, but this is an idiosyncratic use of the term.

IBM: International Business Machines - the company that designed the original PC and is still a leading manufacturer.

IDE: Integrated drive electronics. Refers to a hard disk drive where much of the circuitry that used to be on the hard disk controller card is fitted to the drive unit.

Ink jet: A printer where characters and graphics are formed from a grid of dots (a matrix) produced by fine ink nozzles.

Integer: A whole number.

Integrated package: A minimum of word processor, spreadsheet and database bundled together. Other programs may be included, such as graphics and comms. They may be parts of a single program, or a collection of individual programs loaded from a menu system. Integrated packages tend to be cheaper and less fully-featured compared to buying good-quality individual applications.

Interleave factor: On hard disks describes one aspect of the way information is arranged on the disk surface. The lower the ratio, the faster data can be transferred, with 1:1 being the optimum.

ISA: Industry standard architecture - the design of PC usually classed as an AT.

K: Kilobyte (1,024 bytes).

LAN: Local area network. A network on one site where all devices on the network such as PCs, printers and tape drives are directly connected together so that files and resources may be shared. Also

Laser printer: A printer which uses photocopier technology to output high-quality pages of text and graphics.

LIM EMS: See expanded memory.

Local Bus: The problem with the expansion bus is that, compared with the rest of the PC, it transfers data slowly. This inhibits the performance of some devices that operate via the expansion bus - principally video cards (slow screen update) and hard disk controllers (slow loading and saving of files). Local Bus is, in effect, an additional expansion bus of more modern design that gives greatly increased data transfer rates. It was originally intended for video cards - hence VESA having defined one of the competing standards (VL-Bus) - but hard disk and other cards where speed is important are being produced to fit Local Bus slots.

Cards must be specially designed not only to run in Local Bus slots, but for a particular standard of Local Bus. Beware of PCs advertised as having a couple of VL-Bus slots, but being supplied with an ordinary video card fitted in the conventional expansion bus. You will See no benefit from Local Bus unless the PC has the special video and/or hard disk card to fit it.

Macintosh, Mac: See Apple Macintosh.

Macro: A stored sequence of keystrokes that can be replayed by pressing just one or two keys or by entering a short command. It's a short-cut to save typing. Some applications incorporate a macro facility, and in some cases this has been embellished to the point where it is better described as a programming language.

Mail merge: The process whereby, for example, multiple copies of a letter created with a word processor can have names and addresses read in from a database and inserted at designated points to form personalised correspondence.

Maths coprocessor: A chip inside a PC that speeds up calculations using floating point numbers - numbers with a fractional part. Programs must be specially written to take advantage of the chip if it is fitted. Common maths coprocessors can be numbered 8087, 80287, 80387SX, 80387DX or i487SX depending on the type of CPU they are designed to work with. The i486DX has a coprocessor built in, as does the Pentium, but the i486SX does not.

Mb: Megabyte (1,024K, therefore 1,048,576 bytes).

MCA: Microchannel Architecture. IBM's latest design of PC that it would like to supersede machines based on the XT and AT standards. See EISA. It hasn't really caught on.

MDA: Mono Display Adaptor. IBM's original screen display standard. It could only generate text, and so was unsuitable for the construction of pictures from individual dots.

Memory: Electronic circuits that store programs and data.when they are active. See RAM and ROM. Not to be confused with the hard disk. Memory on the PC is a complex subject for people who aren't technically minded. Read address, byte, expanded/extended memory, high memory and upper memory.

Memory cache: A small area of fast memory (it can be written to or read from quicker than most memory chips) separate from the PC's main memory pool. It is used to store the most frequently accessed sections of the currently running program. Consequently they run more quickly and the program speeds up.

Memory Manager: A program that controls and arbitrates the use by other programs of extended memory. It can also convert extended memory into expanded, and in some cases move some extended memory down into the upper memory area.

MIDI: Musical Instrument Digital Interface. A standard connector and communications technique that allows suitably equipped computers and musical instruments to control each other to greatly expand their musical processing abilities.

Modem: MOdulator/ DEModulator - a hardware device that connects to the PC and allows it communicate worldwide with other computers via the telephone system. A modem translates the 1s and 0s of computer data into a rapid sequence of high and low tones.

Motherboard: The main circuit board in your PC which carries the basic components forming the heart of a computer.

Mouse: A device that can be pushed around your desk to control an on-screen pointer. At least two buttons are used to select menu items and perform actions on objects. Connects either to a serial port or a special mouse socket.

MPC: Multimedia PC. A minimum specification, defined by Microsoft, for PCs intended to run multimedia applications: A 386SX processor, CD ROM drive, MIDI and digitised sound, Windows, plus multimedia extensions.

MS-DOS: Microsoft Disk Operating System.

Multitasking: Running more than one program or doing more than one job simultaneously. Differs from task switching in that multitasking programs are open and running at the same time. A task switcher will switch between applications without closing them, making it look superficially the same as multitasking, but only the currently selected program is doing any work. The others are frozen until you return to them. Windows will multitask or task switch, depending on the circumstances.

Network: A way of linking several PCs together so that they can swap files and share resources such as printers and hard disks. Printing across a network means outputting to a printer on the network rather than one attached to your own printer port.

Optical Character Recognition. The process of turning a graphical image of text, in which each character will be a picture composed of dots, into ASCII text understood by word processors and databases. Text in graphic image format most commonly comes from documents read in by a scanner, or from a fax card. OCR software is often supplied with these devices.

Operating system: A program which is automatically loaded into your PC when it is switched on and provides the A>, B> or C> prompt. When you type a command it either acts on it if it is built in - COPY, for example - or looks for a program of that name on the disk and runs it. MS-DOS is not the only operating system you can run on your PC - OS/2, Windows NT and Unix are more sophisticated examples.

Optical disk: A form of disk drive that involves the use of laser light as part of the recording/retrieval process. There are several competing types, not all of which are commercially available. Some drives mix magnetic and optical techniques (referred to as magneto-optical drives).

OS/2: A modern multitasking, WIMP-based operating system devised by IBM and Microsoft, intended as the successor to MS-DOS. It does, however, have rivals in Windows NT and to a limited extent Unix with other competitors on the horizon.

Parallel port: A socket on the back of your PC that can be used to exchange information with other devices that also have a parallel port fitted. It is usually used with a printer and often known as a Centronics port. It employs a faster technique than that used by the serial port.

Partition: A sub-division of a hard disk made at a much more fundamental level than a directory, for example, which is a high-level structure set up by an operating system such as MS-DOS. Partitions and directories relate in a similar way as do continents and towns. Different partitions might contain different operating systems, their programs and files. Partitions can also be made to behave as if they were different hard disks so on a machine with only one physical drive DOS might recognise drives C, D, E and so on. These would be known as logical drives.

Pascal: A language - used a lot in education - that is powerful enough to be used in commercial programming projects. .

Path: A list of directories through which DOS searches if the program you have asked it to run is not in the currently selected directory. The path can be set up from the DOS command line, but would normally be defined in autoexec.bat.

PC: The IBM Personal Computer, its clones and successors.

PCW: A computer made by Amstrad based on earlier technology than that employed in the PC. Mainly used for word processing, it cannot be used to run MS-DOS or other PC programs.

PCX: A graphics file format.

Pen plotter: Akin to a printer, but works by moving pens over the surface of the paper. Often used in conjunction with CAD software to produce engineering drawings, for example.

Pentium: See CPU.

Peripheral: Strictly speaking any device connected to the core computing circuitry of CPU and memory, for example the disk drives. Usually taken to mean items outside the case, such as printers.

Pixel: Each dot (PICture ELement) on the screen or printer. Every character, line or filled area you see is built from pixels, rather like colouring in squares on graph paper.

Portable PC: A small PC designed to be carried around. Many models have batteries so they can be used on the move.

PostScript: A type of computer programming language which is understood by some laser printers. Commands in PostScript do such things as print text, draw lines and fill areas. A PostScript file is a complete set of instructions that tells the printer how to draw one or more pages.

RAM: Random access memory - the circuits that store a program loaded from disk while it is being executed by the CPU. RAM is also used by the program as a storage area for its data. When the power is removed from RAM, its contents are lost. See ROM. Put more simply, RAM is where programs are stored temporarily when you are running them.

Re-boot: See boot.

Record: See database.

Resolution: A computer display is composed of rows and columns of dots from which all characters, lines and filled areas are built. Resolution is a measure of the number of rows and columns.

On the screen, for example, 320x256 means 320 dots across and 256 high. Printers measure resolution slightly differently. Instead of the total number of dots, it is the number of dots per inch, or dpi. The more dots in an area, the higher the resolution and the crisper the display.

RLL: Run length limited - a method of storing information on a hard disk in which data is compressed compared to MFM to give around 50 per cent extra capacity and faster data transfer rate.

ROM: Read-only memory. Cannot be written to by the CPU but it does not lose data when the power is switched off. Used by hardware manufacturers to incorporate programs and data that must be permanently available into PCs, expansion cards, printers, modems and other devices. Also see RAM.

Root directory: See directory.

RS232: The name of an international standard governing the way a serial port works.'RS232' is often used instead of 'serial port'.

Scanner: A device which scans photographs or other illustrations to create either greyscale or colour images for use in a DTP program, for example.

Screen mode: The PC's display is composed of a fine grid of dots, each of which may be set to one of a finite number of colours. The more dots there are on the screen (higher resolution), and the greater the range of colours available, the crisper and more realistic the image. Unfortunately, higher resolutions and greater colour ranges require more memory for the PC's internal representation of what's on the screen. And because more information is being stored, it takes longer to update the screen.The number of modes available depends on the video card. The fastest option, available on all cards, is text mode. This is a special mode in which the smallest thing that can be changed on the screen is an entire character. This is represented in the screen memory as just two numbers - one to indicate the character, the other its colour. The hardware sorts out what the character should look like in terms of illuminated dots. Contrast this with the graphics modes in which each dot (pixel) has its own number, and there are dozens of dots in a character shape.

SCSI: Small Computer Systems Interface. A general-purpose high-speed multitasking electronic interface used to connect a computer to peripheral devices such as suitably equipped printers and disk drives. Up to seven devices can be joined to one SCSI port.

Sector: See disk.

Serial port: A socket on the back of your PC that can be used to connect it to a computer or other device such as a mouse, modem or pen plotter that also has a serial port. It is used to send and receive information. Also known as RS232. See parallel port.

Shadow memory: Usually refers to RAM in the upper memory area being put to a particular use. In this area live programs that are etched into ROM chips because they have to be permanently available, even if no disk drive is fitted from which they could be loaded. The main example is the BIOS. ROM chips are inherently slow to yield up information, meaning that a program stored in ROM runs more slowly than the same thing stored in RAM. Shadow memory is a system whereby a chunk of RAM is re-located to the same addresses occupied by the ROM, the contents are copied into RAM, and the ROM switched off. The result is that the formerly ROM-based programs now run from RAM, so execute more quickly. It is the two blocks of memory existing at the same addresses, one obscuring the other, that gives rise to the term 'shadow'.

SIM/SIMM: Single in-line memory module - very like a SIP except there are no legs. Instead there are metal strips on the edge of the device which fit into a socket.

SIP: Single in-line package - a chip, or set of chips mounted on a miniature circuit board, with connector legs in one line along an edge.

Sound card: An expansion card which greatly improves the PC's dismal sound capabilities. Essential for full enjoyment of games and music software, and increasingly being used for serious digitised speech applications.

Spreadsheet: A program used to store and perform calculations on figures. It is based on a grid of cells corresponding to the squares on a piece of ruled paper. Each cell can contain explanatory text, a number, or a formula that acts upon the contents of other cells.

Subdirectory: See directory.

SVGA: Super VGA - VGA with extra facilities worth having if your software supports them. Not an IBM standard, but one devised by third-party video adaptor manufacturers.

SX chips: The 386SX is a version of the 386 CPU. It does almost everything a 386 (or 80386DX, to give it its full name) can do, but fits circuit boards using components intended to work with the older 80286 CPU. The result is a cheaper PC which has a 386 PC's special capabilities but runs slower. The 486SX is a version of the 486 CPU (now known as the i486DX). It lacks the 486's on-board maths coprocessor, but retains other improvements of the 486 over the 386. A 487SX maths coprocessor is available.

System disk: A floppy disk that contains copies of essential operating system (DOS) files from which a boot can be performed. System disks are created by adding the /S switch to the FORMAT command - FORMAT A: /S to make the disk in drive A into a freshly-formatted system disk.

System files: Special files, normally hidden from the DIR command, that contain the operating system. The PC loads them when it starts up.

Tape streamer: A device used to keep a copy of files from a hard disk. These back-up files are stored on a tape cartridge which is removed and kept somewhere safe. In the event of files being accidentally lost from the hard drive they can easily be restored.

Text mode: See screen mode.

Track: See disk.

Tracker ball: Rather like a mouse on its back - the device remains stationary and you rotate the ball to move an on-screen pointer.

TSR: A program designed to remain quickly accessible even while another application is running, often by pressing a special key combination known as the hot key. A TSR can stop being active (Terminate) but still remain in the PC's RAM (Stay Resident).

Transfer rate: Usually mentioned in connection with hard disks. Refers to the rate at which data is transferred from the drive to the PC's memory, or vice versa. The larger the number, the faster the drive. This figure is more important than access time.

Typeface: See font.

Upload: See BBS.

Upper memory: Between conventional memory (the first 640K) and extended memory is a gap 384K in size. Parts of it are occupied by hardware such as the BIOS and the video adaptor, but there is unused space that is not fitted with memory chips. A memory manager can take advantage of special capabilities of the 386 and 486 CPUs to relocate some extended memory in this space, where it becomes upper memory.

V22, V23 etc: These are the names of internationally agreed standards applying to modems and refer to the speed at which they can operate. A modem will probably be able to operate at more than one speed.

VDU: Visual display unit - the monitor.

VESA: Video Electronics Standards Association. A group of companies with an interest in the PC's video display (screen), such as SVGA video card manufacturers. VESA aims to define standards where none existed before, and which were causing problems for programmers and users.

VGA: Video Graphics Array. IBM's third stab at a mass-market colour video adaptor. Still more colours and higher resolution than EGA. Until recently the most popular standard on new machines, though SVGA has overtaken it now.

Virus: A program that secretly installs itself in a PC and tampers with the system to ensure it gets run automatically. The virus makes copies of itself and thereby spreads to other PCs, normally via floppy disks. Some viruses have no bad effects while others wipe data from disks or do something else destructive.

WAN: Wide area network - a network that spreads over several sites. Each site will have a local network system (LAN), and talk to the other systems by means of modem or radio link.

WIMP: Acronym for windows, icons, menus, pointer (or windows, icons, mouse, pull-down menus depending on who you listen to). It's the general name for easy-to-use systems like Windows and GEM where the PC's screen imitates a desktop on which there are folders and pieces of paper. Items are represented graphically and selected by moving the pointer and clicking the mouse button. Actions are invoked from menus pulled down from a bar at the top of the screen.

Windows: A program written by Microsoft that runs in concert with MS-DOS to provide a WIMP method of control. It overcomes many of the limitations of unadorned MS-DOS such as being able to multitask and use modern amounts of memory - when a program has been specially written to run from Windows.

WYSIWYG: Pronounced 'wizzy-wig'. An acronym for 'what you See is what you get'. Refers to programs that accurately represent on the screen the appearance of the final printed output. Most DTP programs as well as a smaller number of word processors are WYSIWYG.

XGA: Extended Graphics Array. IBM's newest video adaptor, intended to supersede VGA, but yet to find its way into the mass clone market. SVGA is becoming the standard.

XT: Extra technology - an IBM model designation now generally accepted to mean any PC with an 8088 or 8086 CPU. Also See AT.

Zapf Dingbats: A typeface (See font), designed by Hermann Zapf, that is composed of symbols such as arrows, stars, ticks and crosses. The name comes from on one of Zapf's acquaintances who looked over his shoulder and said something like: 'Yo Hermie, what are all those little dingbats?'.

ZIP file: A file generated by the utility PKzip. See file compression.

INDEX

A

B

C

G

I

L

M

N

P

S

T

V

NOTES